UNHAPPY
TEENAGERS

UNHAPPY TEENAGERS

A Way for Parents and Teachers to Reach Them

William Glasser, M.D.

HarperCollins*Publishers*

HarperCollins books may be purchased for educational, business, or sales promotional use. For information, please write: Special Markets Department, HarperCollins Publishers Inc., 10 East 53rd Street, New York, NY 10022.

FIRST EDITION

Designed by Nancy Singer

Printed on acid-free paper.

Library of Congress Cataloging-in-Publication Data

Glasser, William.
    Unhappy teenagers : a way for parents and teachers to reach them / William Glasser.—1st ed.
        p.   cm.
    Includes bibliographical references and index.
    ISBN 0-06-000798-2
    1. Parent and teenager. 2. Parenting. 3. Adolescent psychology. 4. Choice (Psychology). 5. Control (Psychology) I. Title.

HQ799.15 .G59   2002
649'.125—dc21
                                                        2001051448

02 03 04 05 06 WB/RRD 10 9 8 7 6 5 4 3 2 1

To Jana, Nate, and Julianne

CONTENTS

Contents

PREFACE

On the fourth of March, ABC television presented an Oprah movie featuring a young, single mother's attempts to cope with her beautiful sixteen-year-old daughter, whose crowning glory was her wavy mass of golden hair. There was no male figure in the home. The girl had been told that her father had been killed before she was born. The mother was portrayed as cold, repressed, and prudish.

The story goes on to show the girl falling in love with her warm, seductive high school math teacher who, sensing loneliness, takes advantage and gets sexually involved with her. The movie points out that he was also lonely because his wife had recently left him. As you may suspect, he began his involvement with her by driving her home after school and soon seduced her in his car in a secluded place.

But coincidentally they were seen by her mother's boss, who reported it immediately to her mother as soon as he got back to the office. Her mother came right home, accused the girl of it, and they had a terrible row. The girl defended the teacher, claimed she loved him, and told her mother he loved her, too.

That same evening, the mother went to the teacher's home and confronted him. In order to avoid trouble the teacher immediately offered to leave, saying, "Don't worry, I'll be gone early tomorrow; you'll never see me again and I'll never contact the girl," which he didn't. The mother went home and told the girl what she had done and what he'd agreed to. When the girl defended the teacher and, again, protested their love for each other, the mother threw her down on the floor and cut off her gorgeous hair. The mother was troubled by what she'd done but she still felt it was the right thing to do.

A lot of other things happened to flesh out the plot but, later, the mother revealed her own story. It was much like her daughter's except, unlike her daughter, she had gotten pregnant, and her daughter was the result of that encounter. After a few rocky months in which a few things happened to help the mother see the light, they made up. Love again conquered all.

The above story makes for good TV viewing, but this book is going to give parents of teenagers who have premature sex or get into other difficulties much different advice. In this book, I'll show that the best time to deal lovingly with a love-starved daughter is when the incident happens. Doing what the mother in the movie did could have led to disaster. Suicide would be a strong possibility.

As much as rejection and punishment might seem to be the right thing to do to teach a wayward daughter a lesson, they never are. The real test of the love you have for your child is how you deal with her not when the going is easy, but when you are faced with a situation like this. The stories in this book are aimed at helping you pass the test presented by every serious problem you have with your teenager. More than anything, in times of trouble, your love is desperately needed.

ONE

When You Stop Controlling, You Gain Control

Even though it doesn't seem this way to you, it is no more difficult to get along with your teenager now than it was when he or
she* was younger. Why you can't is the result of how you are
both *choosing* to behave. He's behaving differently because he's
older and feeling his oats. His challenging behavior is normal.

Unfortunately, your choice to do what parents have done
for generations when challenged by a teen, your retaliatory or
controlling behavior, is normal, too. What I will explain in this
book is what I believe you were already sensing before you
started reading. What you are doing or thinking about doing
hasn't worked in the past, it isn't working now, and it won't
work in the future. Still, you keep choosing to do it. You could
record your last argument and when the next one starts, say,
"Why don't I just play the tape of our last row. It'll save us time
and energy and the result will be the same."

As I will explain in this book, as much as you try, you can't

---

*From now on I will use either *he* or *she* when I refer to a teen. I will not
use "he or she," even though that's what I mean.

control an adolescent's behavior when you're not with him and can control only very little when you are with him. What you can control is your own behavior. In fact, as I will explain over and over in this book, yours is the only behavior you can control, so it makes sense to stop doing what doesn't work and start doing what does.

Almost everything I explain will lead you to deal with your teenager differently from the way you now believe you should do. By doing so, instead of seeing your relationship with him deteriorate, you will not only keep whatever closeness you may have now, you'll most likely grow even closer. And as you do, you will be pleasantly surprised by the change in both of you.

Everything I suggest you do in this book is based on *choice theory,* a theory I've created and have used to solve problems like yours since I began to counsel parents and teenagers many years ago. What I've learned is that everyone like you, who can't get along with your teenager (or with one or more of the other important people in your life) is best described as unhappy. This familiar state of mind is present in your teen or any of the other people with whom you are not getting along to the extent you want.

Actually, I believe that, barring grinding poverty, incurable illness, or living under tyranny, unhappiness is the only human problem. Even though I am a well-known psychiatrist, since I've developed choice theory, I have given up thinking of human unhappiness as some sort of a mental illness caused by something mysterious going on in the brain.

None of the parents or teenagers in this book has anything chemically or physiologically wrong with their brains. The problems I discuss are caused by the way either the parent, the teenager, or both choose to deal with their unhappiness. I encourage you to think of the simple, clear, and understandable concept of unhappiness. To become happier, I suggest you use choice theory to improve your relationship with your teenager. You will know when you succeed because you and your child will be happy. You will feel much better because we all know the difference between being happy and unhappy.

When we are unhappy our first thought is that we have to do something about it. For a parent unhappy with a teenager, this almost always means trying to do something coercive to make him change. Threatening, punishing, or bribing will be your most common choices. You may try to find someone like a counselor to help you change your teen's behavior. There is also the remote possibility that you will try to change your own behavior in ways that will, even in this moment of trouble, get you closer to your child. This book will try to persuade parents to change that remote possibility to a strong probability by using the choice theory I'll teach here.

But before I start to explain choice theory, I would like to point out the difference between happiness and unhappiness. When we are unhappy, we are unsatisfied and try to do something *about* it—for example, to change our own life or, more often, to change someone else's life. When we are happy, we tend to be relatively satisfied *with* our life. But then, to feel even better, we may concentrate on doing something more. For example, we may try to widen our circle of relationships or widen our range of achievement, often both. When we are happy our life tends to expand; when we are unhappy our life tends to contract.

As soon as you become unhappy with your teenager, you tend to stop doing things with him and start doing things *to* him, things that I will soon describe as the seven deadly habits. As long as you were happy with your teenager, you did more things with him and encouraged him to do more things for himself. The happier you both are, the more you do with each other. I'm not saying that you have to do the same kind of things with a teenager that you did with him as a preteen but it helps to talk, listen, and share on a different level with this more mature person. Even if you don't do more with him, it seems as if it's more because you feel comfortable when you're with him.

The goal of this book is to help you to change your behavior. This is not a haphazard process. You accomplish it by learning choice theory, the theory of getting along well *with people* and using it to replace what I call the theory of *external control psychology*, which is the theory that most of you have been using in your life and that leads you to do things *to people* that harm your relationships with them. It is the theory that unsuccessful parents use with their teenagers and that has led them to their present unhappiness.

Why You Should Replace External Control Psychology with Choice Theory

If you want to learn more about both choice theory and external control psychology than is explained in this chapter, I suggest you read my comprehensive 1998 book, *Choice Theory: A New Psychology of Personal Freedom.*[*] But in this chapter and the next, concepts will be discussed sufficiently for you to begin to use this information as you attempt to improve your communication with your teenager.

To begin, choice theory explains, we *choose everything* we do. This means that each one of us can control only his own thoughts and actions. By exerting a great deal of coercion we can temporarily control the actions of other people but we can never control their thoughts. And as soon as any person is free

---

*William Glasser, *Choice Theory: A New Psychology of Personal Freedom* (New York: HarperCollins, 1998).

of us, as when she is out of our sight, she can do anything she pleases. How far she will deviate from what you want her to do—and she always knows what you want her to do—will depend on the strength of your relationship. The stronger it is, the more she will behave the way you want her to when she is on her own.

If you can accept the simple but powerful idea that we all choose everything we do, you will have learned a basic choice theory premise. You have choices and your teen has choices. Neither of you is locked into any behavior; both of you can make a different choice and, if you are not getting along well, a better choice is almost always possible. For example, one of the things you will learn in this book is that grounding a seemingly out-of-control teen is rarely the best choice.

Learning that you are choosing what you say and do, and that no one made you say or do it, will help you to stop saying, "She made me do it." No matter what your teen did or said, she didn't make you do or say anything—and vice versa. If you think back to a recent angry interchange you had with your teen, you'll hear yourself repeating what your parents said when they grounded you: "You asked for it." But you didn't ask for it when they grounded you any more than your teen did now. You chose to ground her. Blaming your behavior on her will make it even harder to solve the problem.

I'm sure you've been discovering since you were very small that unhappiness is experienced in many different ways. For example, you may be angry, depressed, anxious, fearful, tense, tired, sick, or even crazy. You may also suffer from severe pain in your head, back, and stomach. It may be difficult to sleep, or you may be tired all the time and walk around feeling as if you're carrying a load on your back. If you are having a lot of trouble with a difficult teen, you know all too well what I'm talking about.

If through what I suggest in this book you can learn to choose more effective behaviors to use with your teen, you will stop feeling the pain and discomfort mentioned above. As uncomfortable as you may be now, feeling better, even happy, is within your grasp if you can learn to make better choices when you deal with her than you're making now.

There is, however, a serious problem you are not aware of that may stand in the way of your making these better choices. That problem is your common sense. It is your common sense, supported by the common sense of people you talk with, that tells you to ground your daughter when she won't come home on time. Common sense may be defined as believing so strongly that something is true that it never crosses your mind to question this belief. What you'll discover as you read this book is that choice theory is not based on common sense, and many of the things I suggest that you do will go against your long-held commonsense beliefs.

Your natural tendency, reinforced by commonsense advice from friends and family, is to think that there's nothing wrong with grounding your daughter, even if that doesn't seem to be working. All you need to do is to apply that strategy longer and harder until it works. For example, if you're denying your son the use of the car for a week, make it a month.

From what you have read so far, all you may agree with is that right now you're unhappy. In fact, judging from years of experience helping parents solve problems with their teenagers, I am certain that if you were sitting here with me now and I was explaining to you why you are so unhappy about your teen's behavior, you'd protest by saying, "I'm not choosing what I'm doing. It's that kid, he makes me crazy. What other choice do I have when he doesn't do a thing I say? He looks at me like I've lost my mind when I ask him a simple question like when are you going to be home or where are you going tonight? Okay, I lose it. I yell, scream, threaten, and punish. What would you do in this situation? Just sit there and do nothing?"

My answer to you is the answer I always give parents: "Learn and use the choice theory, which I'll try to teach you, and you'll rarely find yourself in situations like those you just described." The whole point of reading this book is to learn what you don't know. If you keep doing the same commonsense things your parents did with you, their parents did with them and you're doing with your kids, nothing's going to change.

Be patient. It takes a while to learn to use choice theory. When you do, you'll soon begin to realize that all the people around you, when they are having difficulty with another human being, are choosing what they say and do. They're doing it because they, just like you, believe it's the right thing to do. But as strongly as you think you're right, your teenager thinks you're wrong. To persuade him to consider that you may be right, you will need to be a lot less sure and a lot more willing to listen to his side of the story. To give him some indication that you don't need to have all the power and that sharing some with him may be a good thing to do.

The point of this whole book is that when you have a problem in the way you're dealing with your teenager, your husband, your wife, or any other human being you want to get along with, you will never solve that problem by trying to make the other person see that you are right and he or she is wrong. What choice theory teaches is that the problem you are struggling with is almost never a simple question of right or wrong. It would be so much easier to solve if it were.

Your life is not controlled by a traffic light, stopping on red and going on green. Your life is much more like what happens when, as you approach the traffic light, it turns yellow. There is no certain right or wrong action in that situation. You could run the yellow and get killed by a motorist jumping the red to get away quickly. You could jam on your brakes and get killed by a speeding motorist behind you who expected you to go through the yellow. In either instance, you could be right and be just as dead as if you'd been wrong.

What choice theory teaches—and which I will try to teach you directly, and your teen indirectly through what I teach you—is to take the whole situation between you and him into account. There are indications surrounding the yellow-light situation that can give you information that could help you to make a reasonably good choice.

With you and your teen, the indications are even clearer than with the yellow light. When you disagree, the prime consideration should not be who's right or who's wrong. It should be whether what you are trying to do will preserve or harm the relationship between you and your child. To preserve, even at times to improve, your relationship, sometimes you may have to give in.

Once your teen becomes aware that your giving in is a possibility, she may recognize that her relationship with you is as important to her as it is to you. When she becomes convinced of that, there is a good chance she will stop seeing you as someone who is always wrong while she's always right but in a new light as someone who, above all, wants to keep the relationship between you and her strong.

Learning to respect what the other wants even though you may not agree will accomplish much more with your teen than having each disagreement escalate into a power struggle, even though you win. You will learn to disregard your common sense, which is telling you strongly that *you are the parent, you have the power and you should use it.* Just moving the power axis so it lies somewhere between you and your child will go a long way toward improving your relationship.

The secret of a successful relationship between any two people when the power is unequal is for the person with the most power to do as much as he or she can to show respect for the weaker person's position. Don Juan's advice to would-be seducers—treat a charwoman like a duchess and a duchess like a charwoman—applies to other relationships as well.

As soon as you begin to realize that the relationship between you and your teen has grown strained, it is time to begin to seek a solution, one that attempts to strengthen the relationship by not yielding to the temptation of exercising your power. This is the time to do all you can to respect the position of your teen, even if he seems to be so much in the wrong. Your teen may be weaker but he is not without the ability to do himself and others a lot of harm by showing you that you can't control him at school or anywhere else when he is out of your sight. As I will state over and over in this book, when he is on his own, your only control over him is the strength of your relationship.

What choice theory teaches is that you can win a few battles by punishing him but you'll rarely win the war. Keeping the war going is cutting off your nose to spite your face. If in trying to solve a problem you harm your relationship, you've both lost. For example, how many times in your life have you said something and then immediately thought, I shouldn't have said that. You had that thought because you knew before you said it that you were going to harm your relationship. You were running the yellow light knowing full well that another car was coming through from the other direction.

When you use choice theory, you are always thinking and acting to preserve and strengthen your relationships so that when you come to a difficult situation you can use that strength to negotiate. What you negotiate may not be a perfect solution but it will not be a disaster. It will be enough in between that you don't harm your relationship. Enough that when the crunch comes, you'll still be communicating.

When I dealt with troublesome teenagers, which was often the case in my practice, I employed the strategies that I will both explain and show you in this book. I'll admit it was easier for me than it will be for you because I didn't have to face their anger or experience your frustration. The good news is that the choice theory I will teach you how to practice is neither difficult to learn nor hard to apply. The only thing that may hinder you is that this theory is so new to you that you will have to act on trust at first. Doubt caused by your need to be in control, not your inability to perform, will be your biggest obstacle.

You will also have to be alert; old destructive habits are always lurking in the back of your mind, ready to assert themselves. It may be necessary to push them back in order to become accustomed to using choice theory. However, as new to you as choice theory may be, and as difficult to apply, no possible harm can come from your using any suggestion in this book. Even if something that is suggested here doesn't work, it will do no harm at all to your relationship, since instead of blaming you, your teenager will surely give you a little credit for trying.

TWO

CHOICE THEORY AND EXTERNAL CONTROL DON'T MIX

Why is your common sense so hard to give up? It's because that so-called common sense is an integral part of a world psychology I first recognized when I began to develop the ideas that are the basis of choice theory. While I have given that destructive psychology the name *external control psychology*, I usually drop the word *psychology* and refer to it simply as *external control*.

I say it is destructive because when it occurs in any relationship, it almost always begins what I call the *disconnecting process*. If you are having trouble with your teen, this is the result of a process that's been occurring between you for a long time. To try to better describe this process, I typed the word *disconnect* into my computer's thesaurus. What popped up were words I'm sure you recognize as you struggle to deal with your teenager: *disengaged, separated, uncoupled, disassociated,* and *withdrawn.*

Hasn't every confrontation and disagreement you've been having with your teenager accelerated this process? Is it unreasonable to ask yourself, Wouldn't I be better off to do whatever I can to reverse this process? Because, you know as well as I, unless you do something *far different* from what you're doing now, this disconnection is going to get worse.

In the next chapter, I'll begin to show you some specific strategies for reconnecting with your teen. But first we need to understand how external control is driving both your and your teen's behavior.

First of all, external control is the psychology that, essentially, everyone in the world uses when he or she is having difficulty getting along with another person. You may be experiencing conflict with more than one person, but the way you deal with each case is basically the same. In any disconnecting situation, the person with the most power usually initiates the external control. For example, you use it with your teen; your boss uses it with you. If power is shared equally or close to equally, both people will try to use external control, which is what happens in many marriages. Once the process has started, both parties tend to compete in using it and the relationship grows weaker and weaker.

I use the term *external control* because it is the direct opposite of *self-control*. People who use it spend all their efforts trying to change others and very little effort trying to change themselves. When your teen is doing something you don't want him to do, you tend to waste a lot of effort trying to change him—effort that might be better spent learning new ways to deal with him.

External control is the way of the world. In your whole life, you may never have experienced a situation where someone says to you, "I'm having a problem with what you're doing and I think I have to change what I do or we'll never solve the problem." When you begin to do this in your life, you will have begun to replace external control with choice theory.

From the time we were very small, whenever anyone tried to make us do anything we really didn't want to do, we resisted and tried to escape the control. This resistance led to a power struggle, which always harmed your relationship with the controlling person. Of course, when you were small, you usually lost. That loss led to resentment on both sides: your parents' because they had to struggle, yours because you lost.

Then as you got to be a teenager, you were tired and resentful of always being told what to do. But you also began to feel that maybe you now had enough power to resist successfully. It is this universal resistance to control, and the resentment it breeds between parents and teens, that keeps feeding the discord in any relationship. By now I'm sure you have begun to see that external control is a plague on all humanity.

THE SEVEN DEADLY HABITS OF EXTERNAL CONTROL THAT DESTROY RELATIONSHIPS

While there are actually a few more than seven deadly habits, if you eliminate these seven from your dealings with your teenager, you and he will start to get along better immediately. Unless, of course, the relationship has so deteriorated, it no longer exists; but that is unlikely to happen with a parent and a child. Almost all relationships, except some marriages, can be resuscitated by giving up the deadly habits, even if only one party stops using them. If both are willing to do this, then any relationship, even a marriage, has a good chance of being saved.

The deadly habits are *criticizing, blaming, complaining, nagging, threatening, punishing,* and *rewarding to control* (such as saying, If you do this for me, I'll do that for you.) There is nothing intangible about any of them; they are clear and explicit. Exhibiting them in any relationship will damage that relationship. If you keep doing so, the relationship will be destroyed. The most destructive habit by far is criticizing; next comes blaming, but any of the habits are more than capable of disconnecting you from a person you want to be close with.

Even after the relationship is destroyed, you may still stay together—this frequently happens in marriage—but there will no longer be any chance for happiness. The bright side of difficulty with a teen is that, unlike marriage, you are not locked together. You can go about your business separately when the teen is eighteen; you don't need a divorce or a formal separation. After a period of separation, the relationship may be restored through maturity on both sides and by both parties abstaining from the habits.

As soon as you saw the deadly habits listed above, you probably recognized your use of them with your teenager and, possibly, with a few other people in your life. But from experience, I also know that the idea of giving them up is hard for people to contemplate. If we were together, you might say, "What are you trying to tell me? So, when that kid doesn't obey me, you suggest I do nothing. I don't understand."

You're right, you don't understand. I didn't say, do nothing. I said do something very tangible, something you may not have done before, maybe something you've never done when that teen did something you "knew" was wrong. Give up the habits. This is far more than doing nothing. And, although just giving them up will achieve a great deal, I also suggest that you replace them with what I call the seven connecting habits: *caring, trusting, listening, supporting, negotiating, befriending,* and *encouraging.*

Don't wait for trouble. Start acquiring the connecting habits right away. Almost immediately they will begin to strengthen your relationship. Don't take for granted that your teen will know you love him. Make an ongoing effort to connect with him by encouraging and listening to him. Also, learn to use humor to ease the deadly habits out of your relationship. Joke about the way you used to be and compare it with the way you are now. When she keeps employing one or another of the deadly habits on you, show her what she's doing with humor, not putdowns. Of course, she'll try every one of them. We all had lessons in external control from great teachers.

What may surprise you is that with one group of people you never employ the deadly habits. Those people are your long-term good friends. Except when you're kidding around with them, you'd never seriously criticize, blame, or punish them. You really never get into any of the seven deadly habits with a good friend. But, in the external control world we live in, it's unlikely you will use choice theory with anyone else, and equally unlikely anyone else will use choice theory with you.

I've tested this claim that we behave differently with our friends by surveying quite a few of my students, asking them whether their behavior with long-term good friends includes any of the deadly habits. They think it over and agree; it never does. When I ask why it doesn't, they laugh and say, "If it did, I'd lose them as a friend." I believe they're right because most of us have lost a friend or two through these habits. Sometimes we are able to keep them as friends, but once we've made a serious slip into external control, the friendship is never quite the same.

I've tried to figure out why we continue to give in to the habits, for example, why we keep criticizing when we feel the beginnings of a disconnection. All I can think of is that early in our lives, almost all of us receive a sudden burst of "understanding" that comes about in the following way: From the time we're very small, we try to figure out the right thing to do in almost all the common situations in which we deal with others—for example, being courteous or attentive.

We do this because, in the external control world we live in, any time we make a social mistake we lay ourselves open to criticism, blame, punishment, or any of the other deadly habits. By the time we're twenty to twenty-five years old, we've pretty much figured out what's right for us to do in most social situations.

Then, a little later, after we've pretty much figured out what's right for ourselves, we get this sudden and somewhat overwhelming insight. We say to ourselves something like, You know what—I not only know what's right for me, I know what's right for everybody, especially for the people I'm closest to. While it is possible that we do know what's right for others, unless they agree with us, trying to force this knowledge on them is usually a disaster. With this insight—the sense that *I'm so sure I know what's right for everybody around me, it is just plain common sense*—we begin to sow the seeds that, if left to grow, we will harvest as unhappiness. Very likely, what's going on right now in your life with your teenager is the fruit of those righteous seeds.

What choice theory teaches that makes it so difficult to practice is that not only do we not know what's right for others, very often we don't really know what's right for ourselves. In the last chapter in this book, a man called Fred learns that, and it's a very powerful force in helping him to reconnect with his estranged daughters.

If you look around at your family and friends, you will see that the happiest people are the ones who don't pretend to know what's right for others and don't try to control anyone but themselves. You will further see that the people who are the most miserable are those who are always trying to control others. Even if they have a lot of power, the constant resistance of the weaker people they are trying to dominate deprives them of happiness.

CHOICE THEORY

I've already explained the hardest part of putting choice theory to work in your life: *Get rid of external control and all its baggage such as the deadly habits.* The best way to think of choice theory is as the exact opposite of external control. They have nothing in common. To try to blend the two even a little will harm any relationship in which you attempt this. Because it's the opposite of external control, choice theory is often called an *internal control theory.* As much as external control is a strategy to control others, choice theory is a way to leave others alone and concentrate on controlling yourself so that you stay as well connected as possible with the important people in your life.

Choice theory explains that when we are born we are coded with a genetic task that, although it may not be as urgent as breathing, must be performed if we want to be happy; and we must figure out a way to accomplish it. At the core of that task are five basic needs built into our genetic structure: *survival, love and belonging, power, freedom,* and *fun.* If we can learn to satisfy those needs and not frustrate others in the attempt, we will be happy. The better we satisfy them, the happier we will be. When I talked about happiness and unhappiness in the beginning of chapter 1, what I was referring to was the ability or inability to satisfy one or more of these five needs.

At birth we don't know what these needs are and we may never know what they are but, because we are given the ability to feel good and feel bad, not being able to understand those needs doesn't stop us from trying to satisfy them. While we may have hundreds of different feelings, all of them can be divided into two categories: *pain* and *pleasure.* Or as we frequently say when we refer to how we feel, "I feel good" or "I feel bad," and all of us are well aware of that difference.

We spend most of our lives learning how to behave and, because of our feelings, we pay a lot of attention to how we behave. Basically, any behavior we choose that feels good is satisfying to one or more of the five needs. Any behavior that feels bad or hurts is not satisfying to one or more of our five needs.

As you can now easily see, our need for love and belonging is what drives us toward trying to figure out how to get connected and stay connected with others. Our need for satisfying relationships is as much built into our genes as our need to eat and drink.

But then, unfortunately, we also have to contend with our need for power. Just read the front page of any newspaper and you will see this need well represented in most of the stories about people. Almost all that's written in these stories is about people trying to control others or trying to escape from their control. It is your need for power and your teen's resistance to it that has gotten you into the trouble you may be having with him now.

What happens in our lives is that the need for power and the need for love are often in conflict. You may succeed in keeping your teen in the house when she wants to go out but you will fail in keeping the relationship as strong as you'd like it to be. She will not buy your argument that you are grounding her because you love her. I think it is clear that, if you are to satisfy your need for power, you have to figure out how to satisfy it without losing your connection with the people you need.

The only way we can satisfy our needs for both love and power is to gain the respect, trust, and love of the people in our lives. If we try to control them, we may maintain their love but we will never gain their respect or trust. When we are respected, trusted, and loved, we feel powerful; we neither need nor want anyone to fear us.

One important way in which most of us attempt to gain

power while also satisfying our need for love is choosing to do something with our lives that leads us to feel successful but without having to gain this success at the expense of someone else. One of the most disconnecting problems you can have with your children, especially when they become teenagers, is their not working as hard in school as you would like them to—and very often not as hard as they would like, either.

While it is easy to blame a teen for not succeeding, there are serious flaws in the school system that make it impossible for many students to feel successful in school. Just to mention one of these concerns, as long as we have the ABCDF grading system or its equivalent, very few students who do not get B or higher can feel successful in school.

Why this is so and what the schools can do about it takes up over half my time at present. All I can do in this book is explain what you can do as a parent to help your teen succeed in the schools we have. The most important thing you can do to begin is to try not to make school success the measure of your respect and love for your teen. Your child's school may not grade fairly, but you can be fair to your teenager if you choose to be.

I suggest that you read my recent book *Every Student Can Succeed* (see especially appendix A).* If you agree with what I have to say there, you might make an effort to acquaint your local school with these ideas. There is no doubt in my mind that every student who is capable—I believe that 95 percent of all students are capable—can succeed if the ideas in this book, ideas that cost less than what schools are spending now, are put into practice.

I don't know where our need for power came from, but I believe that somehow or other over the span of evolution people

---

*William Glasser, *Every Student Can Succeed* (privately published by William Glasser Inc., 2000; see appendix A).

who survived learned to do so at the expense of other people. The strong got the food and the weak died of hunger. We are the descendants of the strong. The need for power evolved genetically and has led to the external control world we live in.

But even though the world is dominated by external control, there is still a lot of room for you to put choice theory to work in your life. Acquire your power from doing things that gain the respect of others. If you allow power to dominate your life, you may end up like King Midas with an "obedient" golden statue.

To help us escape from the control of others, the need for freedom was built into our genes. In the United States it became obvious to our founding fathers that this need was so important it needed protection. It was the hope for freedom that attracted so many people to our shores. But people driven by a thirst for power and a belief that they know what's right for everybody else have been reducing our freedom since we became a nation.

In fact, the opportunity to satisfy our need for freedom is not only hard to sustain politically, it may be even more difficult in a family. It is especially hard for a parent of a teen who wants more freedom than the parent believes he can handle. This topic will be covered extensively later in this book.

The needs for survival and fun are easier to fulfill. The need to survive is obvious; that to have fun is not. I believe that having fun, which produces a very good feeling, is our genetic reward for learning. If you ask a child whether she has had a good teacher in her school, as I have done many times, the child will say she has. When asked why, the child will say, "She makes learning fun." This teacher is teaching her to use knowledge and doesn't require her to spend a lot of time memorizing facts that will soon be forgotten. There is no fun in that. This book will include the comments of some teens who think that learning should be fun but go to schools that have yet to get this message.

Recreation is the world's biggest business. But if you look closely at what people spend money for, such as traveling, you will see there is a large component of learning as well as fun in the experience. We are descended from people who learned; the people who didn't learn died out.

The parents and teens who are the focus of this book have no problem surviving; that need has become relatively easy to satisfy in most affluent countries. The problems that you and your teen may be facing will be related to your inability to get the love and belonging each of you wants from your relationship. This is a want that will be directly frustrated if you use a lot of external control. Your teen will also have difficulty satisfying his need for power and for freedom, but if you can maintain a good relationship, these needs can usually be worked out.

As you may realize, your teen's need for fun and freedom will be difficult to satisfy in school. Once they get out of the lower grades, many adolescents begin to hate school. As I've already said, there is not a lot you can do about this, but I will offer some ideas to help you.

As we deal with the teen-parent problems in this book, it will become clear how external control frustrates all of the needs. If it isn't obvious, I'll point it out. What you will learn as the book goes on is that the more you practice the major axiom of choice theory, the better off you will be. That axiom is: Whenever you deal with anyone, even a stranger, you will be better off if you don't do or say anything that will lead to a disconnection between you and that person.

You will almost always know if you're disconnecting, as your genetic need for love and belonging has made you very sensitive to when that is happening. Any disconnecting behavior you choose will be accompanied by a slight, but important, warning, like a still, small voice telling you: *Careful, you may disconnect.* Disregarding this warning has gotten you into some of the trouble you may now be in with your teenager. Avoid the deadly habits and replace them with the helpful connecting habits and you will be on your way to avoiding a lot of trouble.

There is much more to choice theory than has just been said, but that should be enough for now to get you started in this book. As we proceed, I will explain choice theory in greater depth.

THREE

KIM AND JODY

In this chapter and throughout the rest of the book, I will continue to teach choice theory by showing you how to put it to work with your teenager. I'll start with Kim and Jody, a mother and daughter I am very conversant with from my practice. Here, as in the rest of this book, I'll use conversations to help you get the flavor of interacting with your teen. I'll begin with Kim, who will be familiar to many of you as she struggles with Jody, a struggle, I believe, mainly a result of Kim's use of external control.

If you can picture a well-dressed woman in her early forties who was obviously tense and seemed a little uncomfortable to be sitting in my office, that would be Kim. Describing her is not important. If you are in your early forties just think of her as looking like you or one of your friends.

I started in by asking, "May I call you Kim? I'm more comfortable with first names." She nodded, and I went on. "I think the best way for us to begin is for you to tell me the story. You said something on the phone about a teenage daughter."

"To tell you the truth, Dr. Glasser, a year ago I never would've dreamed I'd be sitting here. My daughter, Jody, wasn't an angel but we got along fine. The most trouble I had was her squabbling with Jamie, he's my eleven-year-old, but now that she's in high school it's been a nightmare. I don't know what to do with her, and all the advice I get seems to make things worse. I'm an accountant and tax season is coming up. I'm going to be working seven days a week for almost six weeks. You've got to help me. I'll do anything you suggest."

"Go ahead, tell me a little more. I'm pretty sure I can help you. You're not the only distraught mother in this city; I've helped my share of them."

"You really think you can help me?"

"If you'll do what I suggest, I'm pretty sure I can. But please tell me, what's going on?"

"Look, it happened all of a sudden. A year and a half ago I had a normal thirteen-year-old girl. Like I said, we had our moments but we got along. Then she changed. I could see it coming, my God, you could see it coming a block away. It was physical to start with. I didn't think she suspected what was going to happen any more than I did. In less than two years she went from a girl to a woman. She's just turned fifteen and she has the body and hormones of a young adult. She's taller and more developed than I am. All I can think of when I look at her is Lord, what on earth's going to happen next?"

"She has a boyfriend?"

"Karl's one of the bright spots. He's a good kid. He comes from a home where there's actually a mother and father who, from what she tells me, seem to care for each other. As for Jody and Karl, they're inseparable, he's either at our house or she's over there. But that's good. I'd be a lot more worried if they didn't hang around the house so much. But it's not just her and him. She's in a crowd of fourteen- and fifteen-year-old girls who all hang together when they're not with their boyfriends. And they all have boyfriends. All she does when she's home by herself is talk with them on the phone, day and night. She's stopped doing her schoolwork, all of it. It's such a change. She was always a good student. In middle school she was on the honor roll. Now she has this attitude, if you know what I mean. School sucks, the teachers suck, and algebra sucks the most of all. It's boring, boring, boring. She refuses to do homework, and her grades in the academic subjects have fallen to C's except for a D-minus in algebra. She has one elective, art. She likes art but, for her, school's just for socializing."

"Okay, I get the school picture. But something else you're real concerned about brought you in here."

"Well, my worry is the parties. They're every Saturday night, always at a house where no adults are home. She tells me what goes on. There's easy access to alcohol and marijuana and she keeps dropping hints about other drugs. And there's sex. No orgies or anything like that but sex is going on between the steadies."

"I'm surprised she tells you so much. Do you think it might be her way to brag about her new maturity but still try to assure you she isn't involved in the sex and drugs?"

"That might be it. I've thought about it and I keep telling myself it's a good thing she's so open with me. But I'll also tell you that when she gets to talking, I'm not all that sure she's making any real effort to resist what she's telling me about. I have a feeling that the one who's doing the resisting is Karl. When I said he was the bright spot, at least he's kept her from smoking. He's an athlete; he doesn't smoke or do drugs as far as I know. Almost all of her girlfriends smoke, and I get the feeling that smoking for young girls who look like her is the beginning of sex and drugs. I don't mean smoking causes those problems but it's a sign of rebellion, a sign I'm a big girl now. I asked her if any good students she knows smoke and she just made a face. Do you think you can help me get her back to working in school?"

"If I'm able to help you, it'll help with everything. Not at once, it'll take time. But how about your life? From your comment about Karl's parents, I gather you're divorced."

"He left me five years ago for a younger woman. Not really that much younger, but I guess when you're thirty-eight, a twenty-eight-year-old is a lot younger. I don't want to bore you with the gory details. Read 'Dear Abby,' there it is every day. He has a new family and has pretty much abdicated all parental responsibility for our two kids. Jody is totally confused. She loves him and she hates him. She detests his new wife; she'll have nothing to do with her new little brothers. He used to pick her up and take her for the weekend but, since she matured, she gives them such a hard time he wants nothing more to do with her. What she did when she used to go there, she even did it in front of her, was refer to his wife as 'the slut.' My problem is I can't help liking her for it, and I guess she senses my approval and enjoys doing it. A couple of years ago she baby-sat for them a few times but now she absolutely refuses. She says, 'All the slut wants from me is to help them out. He doesn't love me and the slut hates me.' The upshot is he won't even pay child support for her anymore because of the way she acts around them, so I'm in court half the time about that. And my lawyer says I might lose. But Jody tells me I shouldn't worry. She'll go out and work if I need the money. He still pays for Jamie and Jamie treats him fine. That's what the last big fight was about. She told Jamie he shouldn't go over there, and Jamie told her she ought to be nicer and then they got into it. But Jamie needs her. He's always trying to get her attention, but he does all the wrong things to get it. She complains to me that I favor him, which is true, because around me he acts like an angel. I guess he figures that by contrast, he looks pretty good. And actually, he does."

"What's her major beef right now?"

"All my rules. Mostly about school and her constant use of

the phone. And my punishments, grounding her weekends. Once I even threatened not to let her see Karl, but that was a mistake. She went to her room and wouldn't leave. She wouldn't go to school, she wouldn't eat, she wouldn't talk. Karl called me. He was frightened. He begged me to let him at least come over. I gave in. Do you think I did the wrong thing?"

"I'd rather we didn't get into right and wrong. Preaching right and wrong is not much help with kids like Jody."

"You can say that again. I do everything right and it always comes out wrong."

"Can you give me an example?"

"It's the only rule I've been able to cling to. I've allowed her to go to the parties as long as she's with Karl and she's home by eleven-thirty. But now she's pushing for twelve-thirty. I don't want to give in but I'm not sure I can hold out. She tells me she's just not going to come home and I can't do a thing about it."

"Have you done anything to get help besides seeing me?"

"I went to a counselor for one session, but what he suggested was for me to get her father more involved even though I told him that when she's with her father, it's worse. She comes home more out of control. Besides, I can't afford this unless it's pretty quick. I've got insurance for five visits. Money is tight. I work full-time as an accountant, but I'm not a CPA and I get paid peanuts compared to the men. I don't know what I'm going to do if he isn't ordered to pay her child support."

"Do you have any help from anyone in your family?"

"My dad's dead; my mother divorced him when I was in college. He drank. I worry about Jody drinking. My mother still works and has a busy life. She's not really any help. When she does come over, she makes no effort to hide her preference for Jamie, which only adds to my problems. I'd rather she didn't come and mostly she doesn't. Jody really has no adult in her life except maybe her art teacher, who does what she can to be supportive. It's easy for her because, thank God, Jody has some talent and she works in that one class. Her art teacher told me Jody admits she loves me when they've had their little talks. I wish a few more teachers were like that art teacher. She really cares. All I can say is that every time I try to talk with Jody I seem to be losing more ground. I've about stopped bringing anything up except the weather. And even there it's gotten to the point where, if I say it looks like a nice day, she frowns."

WHAT SHOULD KIM DO?

I think it's clear what Kim's problem is. Jody's decided that Kim doesn't understand her and so the best thing for her to do is shut down. She's the kind of young person who might benefit from seeing a counselor, but this book is aimed at teaching parents how to deal with their teen without professional help or with very little. What I'll do now is finish this chapter by taking Kim through a choice theory interaction with Jody. As you read it, put yourself in Kim's shoes even if your teenager has a different problem. My point as I describe the following conversation is for you to begin to see that this choice theory interaction may be a lot different from any you've had with your teen and certainly different from any Kim has had with Jody for a long time.

Basically, I'll guide Kim in the same direction I'll guide all the parents who read this book. The purpose of this guidance is improving their relationships with their teenagers. The relationship Kim has with Jody is not hopeless. She still has a connection with her, but it's much weaker than it was a year ago. My job is to teach her to strengthen it by removing the seven deadly habits of external control from their relationship.

Kim's immediate task is to face the reality that she can only control her own behavior, which mostly means what comes out of her mouth. When Jody is gone from the house, Kim has no direct control over her. But she has some indirect control, which is proportional to how strong her relationship with Jody is. The more she can strengthen that relationship, the greater is the chance that Jody won't engage in the self-destructive activities that go on at the parties that Kim is so worried about.

She certainly doesn't have to lecture Jody about what she's doing wrong or contemplating doing wrong. Jody has known all along that Kim doesn't want her to drink or use drugs or have sex with Karl or anyone else. Kim may not be aware of this but Jody is also watching her closely, so the more circumspect Kim is about her own life, the more Jody will respect her mother's concern about what she may be tempted to do.

Since the activity of any teenager is tempered by her relationship with responsible adults, everything Kim does and says from now on should not be anything that might weaken her connection with Jody. Instead, she should do all she can to strengthen their present connection. She should keep in mind that she doesn't have that far to go; she had a good relationship with Jody before she entered the ninth grade, so she and Jody are still connected. It takes years, even a lifetime, for a child to disconnect from a parent as caring as Kim.

As soon as she can, perhaps this coming Saturday morning, she might try to have her first choice theory conversation with Jody. It would be a good idea to figure out a way to get her son, Jamie, out of the house for a few hours so that she could prep that conversation by making herself and Jody a good breakfast or, if Jody isn't up for breakfast, a good lunch. Kim should sit down and eat with her and as they are eating, start in by saying, "I've been thinking about our relationship and I'd like to have a little talk with you."

Jody will hear her but she may not respond. As far as she's concerned, this will be just another in a long line of external control conversations she's had to put up with since she entered high school. Kim shouldn't ask for her attention. That's just additional external control. She should continue by saying, "I'm worried that I've been trying to run your life since you got to high school and I'd like to talk about it. . . . Do you get the feeling I'm trying to run your life?"

"What do you mean do I get the feeling? You're my mother."

"Are you saying that because I'm your mother, I have the right to keep after you about school?"

"What are you talking about? I don't get it. What do you want me to say?"

Kim has her interest now, should go ahead and say, "Okay, I'm always after you about your grades. Every day, I ask you about your homework. Is it okay if I don't do that anymore?"

What I have been trying to show is that Kim has no control over Jody's grades or whether she does her homework, unless she's prepared to sit with her and try to make her do it. But if she does that, she'll quickly weaken their connection further over something that's not as important as what she does when she goes to the parties. Talking first about schoolwork and homework without using any external control is a good way to start, since doing poorly in school is more easily corrected than any of the things she could get into at the parties, or elsewhere. So here Kim can give ground and not really risk that much. She may even gain a little because Jody can't blame her for nagging and use that as an excuse not to do the schoolwork. What this will also accomplish is to get her attention. Jody will be interested in where this conversation is going, and Kim will suddenly seem a little more important to her.

"You mean you're not going to bug me anymore about school?"

"Nope, I'm finished. If you want me to help you, I'll be glad to help. But for the rest of this year, school is up to you."

"I don't believe you."

"I'm not asking you to believe me. If I start bugging you, call me a liar. The most I might do is ask you to show me some of your artwork. But even that's up to you. If you don't want to, don't."

What Kim is telling her is that she appreciates Jody's art, she's actually proud of it. Saying this will help Kim to strengthen their connection and encourage Jody to go on with this conversation. Also, there will be the very subtle hint that Kim would like to be proud of other schoolwork, but she's not going to come out and say anything like that directly.

Since there is no problem with her art, Jody says, "I like to show you my drawings. You know I like to do that."

"Please do, but don't worry that I'm going to look at them then start in like I usually do about the rest of your schoolwork, because I won't. Anyway, now that I've brought up the subject of not bugging you, is there anything else you'd like me to stop bugging you about?"

"Jamie. You're always after me to be nicer to him. He drives me nuts. He's such a brown-noser! All he does is suck up to you, how can you stand it? . . . I hate him."

"That's a good suggestion. I think I do baby him too much. He's old enough to take care of himself. All I ask is you don't hit him. I can't stand the screaming."

"But he keeps bugging me."

"Walk away, yell at him, curse him, threaten him, even sit down and play with him for a few minutes. Do anything you want except hit him. I can't deal with that. How about your room? I'm always after you about cleaning up your room."

"I'll clean it up. I've been telling you I'm going to do it."

Jody's saying this is a little recognition that maybe Kim has a point about the room. Kim might use this recognition as an opportunity to offer Jody some help. "Would you like me to help you? I'll bet in no time if we work together, we could get it all cleaned up."

"I'll do it myself. It's okay."

Jody's not ready to accept help, but she probably appreciated the offer. Whether she cleans it up or not, Kim shouldn't say anything more about the room. She has to give Jody a chance to be responsible but, if she does clean it up, Kim shouldn't acknowledge the effort. Praising her for doing something she knows she should do is like rewarding her to control her, the seventh deadly habit. Stopping the nagging about the room is enough.

Kim might then say, "How should we handle the phone? A woman from the office tried to call me the other night and my cell phone wasn't working. I guess I forgot to charge the battery. She couldn't get through."

"Could you get me a cell phone? All my friends have cell phones. Then I'd never be on the line."

"Would you find out how much they cost? Why don't you ask your friends?"

"You'd pay for it?"

"I'd pay half if it's not too much. If you'd do a little baby-sitting, you could make enough to pay the rest. After the kids you're sitting for are asleep, you could talk on their phone and save your cell phone time. Tell them you might use their telephone and give them your cell phone number so they can always reach you."

This may seem like a lot of talk about a phone, but it's worthwhile because it was a good talk about a problem that can be easily solved. Now that she's going out, Kim would want Jody to have a cell phone anyway. It also gives Kim a chance to talk about something important to her without using any external control. The more she can figure out things to talk about with Jody, the more that allows both of them to escape from external control. By now, Jody will relax. The initial tension she always shows when Kim starts a serious conversation will be defused. Kim shouldn't worry that she's made a few concessions; she's had the opportunity to talk with Jody in a way she hasn't done for a long time.

Now Kim might continue to talk for a while about anything that interests her and Jody. Clothing, makeup, music, what dances they are doing at the parties. After Kim feels Jody is comfortable and not defensive, she might shift gears to a more important topic. Or she may feel they have talked enough for now. That would be up to Kim. But for the sake of this book, let's assume she has made the connection, and so let's go ahead and use this new comfort level between them to explore an area that really concerns her. But, believe me, it concerns Jody, too. It's what Kim is trying to prevent by giving up the deadly habits as she deals with Jody. She wants to reduce the chance that Jody will do anything self-destructive like taking drugs or having unsafe sex because she's angry at her mom.

Since it's Saturday, Kim might start by saying, "How about tonight? What's your plan for tonight?"

"There's a party. What really bugs me is Karl and I are going and I have to be home by eleven-thirty. What's the big deal about one more hour. All the kids look at me like I'm weird when I leave."

"What time do you plan to get there?"

"I don't know. Nothing really gets going till ten. We're going to a movie first."

"I've got an idea. Maybe we could work something out. What time do you think you could be home? I don't like arguing with you. I think I could give a little."

Here you may disagree with me and think I'm doing the wrong thing by negotiating what many parents believe is non-negotiable. But remember, Kim has no control over Jody when she's not home except what she may gain through improving their relationship. It's not a question of what's right or wrong; it's a question of what control you have or don't have. This talk has already strengthened their relationship. When you give up external control, this getting closer can happen fast. What I'll suggest now is a way to get more connected with her when she's out of the house at a party or really anywhere out of Kim's sight. Kim is now more open to new ideas. She won't refuse what I'm going to suggest, as she would have before making this breakthrough with Jody. She'll listen.

Kim's use of choice theory in this conversation has gotten Jody thinking. She's no longer focusing only on what she wants. She's now having a glimmer of a thought about what Kim wants and realizing that her mother may have a point in being concerned.

Jody finally ventures, "Would it be all right if I came home at twelve instead of eleven-thirty?"

Jody wants twelve-thirty but she isn't asking for it—another sign that giving her a choice doesn't mean that she'll pay no attention to what Kim wants. The more choices you give a teen, the more she may consider a little less than what she wants. That's why she said twelve instead of twelve-thirty. That kind of thinking is what maturity is all about.

Kim might say, "That would be fine if you'd do one thing. Karl has a cell phone with him when you go out, doesn't he?"

"Sure, his parents make him take their cell phone whenever we go anywhere at night. I told you that, don't you remember?"

"I'm sorry. I guess I forgot. Could you do this? Call me at eleven and tell me that you're fine, that I shouldn't worry and that you'll be home at twelve. If you don't call, I'll expect you home at eleven-thirty. Is that okay?"

"Yeah, fine. I can do that."

The thinking behind this approach is that even though Kim is giving her another half hour, she's making a connection with Jody late in the evening and giving Jody a chance to tell her she's fine. Just saying she's all right to her mother helps Jody feel more connected, so it's less likely she'll do anything wrong. Also, Karl will be right there with her when she calls, and he'll make sure to get her home and not risk losing the extra half hour they've gained. When she calls, Kim should tell her to have a good time and to be sure to wake her up when she gets home, she'd like to say hi. Kim should also tell her it's something she always wanted when she was a girl, but Grandma didn't like being woken up. All Kim will want are a few words and a little hug before she goes back to sleep.

There are many other concerns that Kim has with Jody, but the one we have explored is enough for now. Review how Kim handled the situation and contrast it with how you've been doing this with your teenager. There was nothing I suggested that even hints at external control. If you can follow this same strategy, you may have as rewarding a conversation with your teenager as Kim had with Jody.

If the curfew times I suggested are too late, all you have to do is adjust them to your own needs; the method is the same. It's up to you to determine what you will agree to, where you will draw the line, but be careful not to ask for too much. If you do, you'll end up getting less because you will have weakened your connection with her. The connection at this stage in the relationship will keep shifting between weaker and stronger. It will take a lot of choice theory to get it to the point where it's strong and stable.

I can also hear you asking yourself, How can I turn her education over to her? School is far too important. She'll do even less than she's doing now. The reason underlying my suggestion is that if you turn her school over to her, you will defuse the school issue that is muddying the water right now and which you can't really do anything to clear up. We will reintroduce the school issue and the choice theory way of dealing with it in some of the following chapters.

FOUR

KEN AND JOHN

Ken is a well-respected cardiologist with whom I play tennis regularly every Saturday. He's aware that I practice a psychology I call choice theory and that I've written books on it. But he hasn't asked to read any of the books, and it has never been more than a passing subject in our conversations. I have been more and more aware of the fact that he knows next to nothing about what I do because for years he's been complaining about his son John, who is now almost seventeen. He has an older son and daughter who are models of what he thinks children are supposed to be, but he is at his wit's end with John, a late-in-life surprise, born when his wife was forty-five and he nearly fifty. When I told him I was writing this book, he laughed and asked if he could be in it.

I said, "Ken, I have no intention of leaving you out. If ever anyone needed to read a book advising a frustrated father how to get along better with his son, it's you."

He sighed and agreed, saying, "Bill, I have some idea of what you believe in but I won't accept it. If I can't figure out how to motivate that kid, he's down the drain."

"If there is anything in your life you've figured out, it's what to do with John. You've had it figured out since he was in kindergarten. For years I've been listening to what you're trying to get him to do and for years I've been asking you if it's working. So I'll just ask again, Ken, is it working?"

"You know it isn't working but you never tell me what else to do."

"We've been through this too many times. You don't like what I tell you, so I gave up telling you anything ten years ago. You only want me to tell you what you want to hear. That's what everyone wants when what he's been doing isn't working."

"So now you're going to write what none of us will do in a book?"

"I'm going to give it a try. Maybe it'll make more sense when you see it written down. God knows it's needed. There's no shortage of men who are disappointed in their children. You all have the same problem. It's your children who aren't the same, they're all different. I think you got lucky with John."

"I'm lucky to have a kid who won't work in school. A kid who's smart as a whip and never gets a grade above a B. A kid who goes to the local dump they call a high school when I want to send him to a prep school where he'd get a real education. Hell, he won't even take the SATs. He says all he needs he can get at the local community college. The only thing he's interested in is playing bridge. He's on the Internet playing bridge with people from all over the world. Do you know what name he uses so he can get into top games? I just found out."

I shook my head to say I didn't know.

"Smartass. That lazy kid calls himself Smartass and everybody wants to play against him or with him. I can't get over it."

"I like it. I think he is kind of a smartass. He's figured out how to handle you a lot better than you've figured out how to handle him."

"How can you say that?"

"You've told me how happy he is, especially since he's met that girl, Alexis. All you do is complain about him, but does he ever give you a hard time? From what you've told me, never. You keep telling me he loves you and he's a real nice kid. That's why I think you're lucky. Almost all the sons of men who pick on them like you pick on John hate their fathers. You've been telling me how much you like to watch all the football and basketball games with him. Very few sons love a father like John loves you."

"Okay, he loves me but he still gives me a hard time. His whole life gives me a hard time. He could be a top-notch doctor or lawyer. He could be anything he wants."

"He's already everything he wants. And a smartass to boot."

"I know he loves me. He loves his mother. He loves his grown brother and sister. He loves his girlfriend, Alexis, and his grandmother. But if he loves us why can't he do more with his life? Alexis works her head off in school, she wants to be a lawyer. I thought she'd motivate him but he just tells her he's amazed at all the schoolwork she does. I've talked to her. She just says, leave him alone. Bill, he knows what I want and he doesn't do a damn thing about it. When I get so exasperated and start yelling at him, he gives me a hug and tells me to calm down. He says, 'Dad, we all love you. Just relax, everything is okay.' But it isn't okay. How did I ever get a kid like him?"

"Yeah, a kid who doesn't drink, smoke, or use drugs. A son who's never been in trouble in his life. A son who gets almost all B's in school. A son who has an after-school job in the market and makes almost all of his own spending money. You've got a real dud in John. Give it up, Ken; you can't control him. Start trying to control yourself."

"What do you mean, control myself? I do control myself."

"I guess I should have said, control yourself a little better. You're after him all the time. You choose every word that comes out of your mouth. Are those words doing you or John any good? Does it make you feel good to yell the same thing over and over at him about college? Ken, you can't control John, even though you've been trying his whole life. The miracle of it is he still loves you. Does it ever cross your mind that all along he's really been controlling you? You're nowhere near chips off the same block, his block's stronger."

"You're saying that kid is stronger than I am. Look at all I've done; he hasn't done a damn thing except learn to play bridge."

"If he doesn't do what you want, then all the good stuff he does doesn't count? He's even a good tennis player. He's been beating you since he was thirteen, and he hardly ever plays."

"That's just it. He is good. If he'd put a little more into tennis, he could be junior champion at this club."

"I guess he has no desire to be the junior champion. He enjoys tennis, that's enough for him. Tell me, who's happier right now, you or him?"

"He is, but it isn't right. He shouldn't be so happy."

"He may be happy, but I think he cares a lot about your happiness. And he's figured out something very few people ever figure out. You certainly haven't."

"What haven't I figured out?"

"He's figured out that if your happiness depends on him doing something he doesn't want to do, he isn't going to do it. A lot of kids do things to make their parents happy and they end up miserable. I think you could figure out how to be happy with him if you wanted to. Everyone else seems to be able to do it, why not you? I'm sure he'd like you to get off his back, but he's not about to stop loving you because you won't."

"I don't know what you're talking about. He should worry about me being unhappy and do what I tell him to."

"Everyone I see in my office is unhappy, and they're all just like you. They keep telling me that their happiness depends on what someone else does. A woman came to see me yesterday all upset because the guy she's been living with for two years won't marry her. She can't control him any more than you can control John, but she doesn't want to give up trying. But this woman's problem is a lot easier than yours. She can learn to get along without a guy who doesn't love her. I can help her with that. But you can't learn to get along without your son. You're his father, you'll never be able to do that."

"Are you saying I'm so screwed up I need psychiatric treatment?"

"I don't tell anyone they need psychiatric treatment. But the world is full of unhappy people who think they can't be happy unless someone else does what they want. You're a big-shot cardiologist. You see these dissatisfied people every day. Do you think that unhappiness has anything to do with their heart trouble, or is it all bad diet and lack of exercise?"

"No, that's been known for two hundred years. Almost all chronic illness has a lot to do with unhappiness."

"Isn't there some kind of a personality that goes along with heart trouble? Who's closer to that personality, you or John?"

"You're talking about what we call the type A. Or maybe it's better just to call them control freaks. John's so far from type A, he's type Z. But am I a control freak because I want my son to get a good college education? I don't want to have to take care of him for the rest of his life."

"I realize you do a lot for him. But did you push him to go to work in the market? Aren't you surprised he's so responsible about that job? He doesn't really need the money. What does he do with it, do you know?"

"I really don't. I guess he buys some clothes and he spends it on Alexis. But one thing he does do is every other week he buys me a can of tennis balls for our Saturday game. He started doing it as soon as he went to work in the market."

"Do you take them?"

"What do you mean? Of course I take them. I love him and I'm smart enough to take them graciously."

"I'm sorry, Ken. I shouldn't have asked you that. But I feel better now that you've told me you take them graciously. I've really enjoyed this little talk. I'd like to put it in the book, but I won't until I let you read it."

"Dad, is something wrong? The ball game's almost over and you've hardly said a word. You're not angry at me, are you?"

"No, John, I'm not angry at you. I love you. But lately I've been wondering what you think about me. Do you think I love you?"

"Dad, I don't think you love me—I *know* you love me. Why shouldn't you love me? I love you. We've always loved each other. You're my dad."

"But the way I treat you?"

"What way? You've always treated me the same. We watch the games, we play a little tennis. You're great with Lex. You love Mom. None of the kids I know have a dad who cares more about them than you care about me. I know you're busy and you don't have much time for me. It's okay, Dad, I know you love me."

"C'mon, John, you know what I'm talking about. The way I talk to you. I come on as if you don't do anything right."

"Dad, it's the way you are. You know what's right for the whole world. I don't think you're ever gonna change. As long as we keep watching the games and play a little tennis, I'll be fine."

"What I'm trying to tell you is I don't want to be the way I am. I don't want to keep telling you that you're not the kid I want. I can't help thinking, why aren't you like Alexis? She wants to make something of herself. You don't want to make anything of yourself. It bugs me. I'm trying to tell you how I feel."

"Dad, it's okay to feel the way you do. I know I'm not the kid you want. I may never be the son you really want. But keep after me if you want to. It's okay. It's your keeping after me that tells me you care."

"I do love you. I'm just ashamed of myself for being on your case so much. I feel better talking about it."

"I do too, I really do. I like you telling me you love me. But please don't think you're wrecking my life because you're after me all the time. You aren't. Believe me, Dad, I'm happy. You're all bark and no bite. I don't feel the least bit like I have to do what you want me to do. I'm not you. I'm never going to be like you and you're never going to be like me. We're different. I accept it. Lex's a lot different from me, too. She does all the things you want me to do but we get along fine. We talk a lot about how different she is from me but we care for each other and we accept it. Dad, do you think Lex is happy?"

"Of course she's happy. She's doing all the right things. Why shouldn't she be happy?"

"Maybe she should be, but she's not. We're both in the eleventh grade and she's worried she won't get into Stanford Law School. . . . She's five years away from any law school and already she's worried about Stanford . . . Just between you and me, Dad, I don't think she's even close to having what it takes to get into Stanford Law. I haven't said anything but I think she knows it's a lost cause. I tell her she's doing okay; forget about Stanford. Isn't that good advice? What would you tell her?"

"I agree, it's good advice."

"But if that's good advice, what do I do about you? You're miserable because I'm not like you. What's wrong with me being happy the way I am? I'm doing okay in that high school.

Believe me, I'm not throwing my life away just because I have no desire to be in AP classes or to take the SAT. All they do in those classes is memorize a lot of crap that they forget right after the test. They're so worried about forgetting something that a lot of them cheat. I don't cheat. You want me to compete in classes where kids cheat right and left. Lex tells me all about what goes on in those classes. If you don't believe me, ask her. I can't see the sense of memorizing a bunch of stuff you're going to forget. What for? You know what I've been doing this year? I've told all my teachers I won't memorize anything for a test unless they can explain why. I tell them instead I'll be happy to answer any essay questions they want to ask me, and they do it. A few of my friends have joined me and we're learning more than they do in the AP classes. I've asked Lex and she agrees."

"You never told me anything about that."

"Dad, we've never had a talk like this. If you hadn't started in tonight, we never would have. All you've ever wanted for me is to get A's in AP classes and ace the SAT. You've never even thought about what I've just explained."

"But why don't you get A's if you're learning that much?"

"They won't give us an A because we won't follow the rules. It doesn't matter that we're learning a lot more. Dad, the whole system's crazy, and that's the system you want me to go along with."

"But I could do something about that. I know the president of the school board. He's one of my patients."

"If you make a fuss, you're going to get those teachers into hot water and wreck the whole thing. Let it go. Isn't backing out of my life what we're having a talk about?"

"But I never knew."

"How could you know? Who would tell you? Kids don't

talk to parents who know it all. I never saw you say two words to Grandpa when he was alive. Is that the way you want me to be? This is the first time we've ever talked except about football and basketball. You've had my whole life planned since I was in nursery school. If I wasn't so sure you loved me, I might be a drugged-out mess like a lot of the kids in that school. I'm not even sure I'm going to go to junior college. I may take off a few years and play bridge. Smartass is a pretty good bridge player and getting better. There are ways to make money in bridge; people will pay for a good partner."

"John, I know this sounds like lines from a bad play, but it's really hard for me to say this: I've been a fool."

"Dad, you haven't been a fool. You did what you thought was right. I'd have been a fool if I'd gotten angry at you and used it as an excuse to throw my life away. I talk to a lot of kids who are messing up and blaming it all on their parents."

"But how have you figured all this out?"

"I had a role model.

"What do you mean?"

"You, Dad. I figured if you still loved me when I didn't do anything you wanted, I could love you if you didn't do anything I wanted. I figured that out when I was a little kid. It's not only me. Kids aren't stupid; we figure things out. We don't want to wreck our lives any more than you do. As long as we're loved, most of us come out okay. Lexi's figured this out, too. I think it's what got us together. She's not working so hard to become a lawyer because of her father. It's what she wants. You know her father's a lawyer. He didn't even go to a top law school. Now all he does is pressure her about Stanford Law. She lets that bother her, but I've been working on it and she's a lot better. Her mother and father love her. I'm teaching her that their pushing is their problem, not hers. But let me ask you a question: Why have you kept loving me when I haven't done what you want me to?"

"I can't answer that question. I've thought about it a lot. All I can say is I always have. And really it hasn't been that hard. You've always been such a nice kid no matter what I've said. All the men I know are pushing their kids, and a lot of them are having trouble with them. They love their kids, too. What made you turn out this way?"

"Look, Dad, you're not the only person in my life. Mom was always supporting me and telling me you love me. She said you love her but you're just a born know-it-all. It hasn't wrecked her life, and she advised me to put up with it and not let it wreck mine. Just love you and be nice to you and do what I think is right. It's been good advice. I guess you can blame a lot of my niceness on Mom. And if you don't mind, Dad, I'm going to try to marry a woman like Mom and treat her better than you've treated us."

"But Mom's got it wrong. I'm not that way with her."

"Dad, you're that way with the tropical fish. . . . But there's another reason, too. Alexis loves me. I know you like her, but do you have any idea how we feel about each other? Has Mom talked to you about us?"

"She's told me you cared a lot about each other."

"That's all?"

"What more is there?"

"There's a lot more. Mom knows about it. But you don't. She was scared you'd have a heart attack if she told you. But as long as we're having this talk, I thought it would be a good idea to clear the air by telling you what's going on. I'm not comfortable with Mom knowing and you not."

"This thing with Alexis is serious?"

"I don't know if *serious* is the right word but I think you could say we're serious right now. Were you ever in love when you were sixteen?"

"I was in love a few times when I was young. I didn't marry Mom until I was a resident; I was thirty years old."

"When you were very young, were you ever so in love that you had sex with the girl? Or maybe you wanted to but the girl didn't want to. You love me, help me with this. Please, Dad. I can see you tensing up. I don't need a lecture or being told what to do. That won't help me or Alexis."

"John, I was eighteen before I had sex. It was with a girl I loved. I met her at the end of my freshman year at college."

"What happened?"

"We were together for three years. We broke up when I went off to medical school. She wanted to get married and I didn't. I was really upset."

"Lex and I have been making love for six months. A year from September she's going off to college. We know we're going to be separated then. We talked it over and decided to go ahead. That's where we are. I just wonder if you'd like to say anything. She loves you and respects you and I know you care for her. I told her I might bring this up with you and she said she trusts you. Dad, I love her. She's helped me to deal with you. I just wonder if you have anything to say."

"Do her parents know?"

"It's hard to say. They know we're together a lot and we care for each other. I'm sure they suspect something. But Mom's the only one who knows."

There was a long pause and then Ken said, "I guess it comes down to, Do I love you?"

John just kept looking at Ken. He didn't say anything.

"She's on the pill?"

John nodded.

"Mom thinks it's okay?"

"No, Mom thinks it's wrong. She thinks we're way too young."

"Do either you or Alexis think it's wrong?"

"We've tried to stop but we can't. She wants me to work hard and try to get into the university with her. Where education is concerned, she's on your side."

"I don't know what you expect me to say. I agree with Mom. I agree with Alexis. But you want something more from me?"

John nodded.

"You want me to tell you I love both of you."

"Yes, that's what we want, Dad; it's important to us."

"You want us to talk with her parents."

"No, all we want is your love. We've got Mom's love. We may mess it up but we want to work it out ourselves. If we want help, we'll ask you for it."

Another long pause.

"John, I need a hug. A real one. Not a football or basketball hug."

The next time we played tennis, Ken couldn't wait to talk. He filled me in on all you just read. Then he turned to me and said, "What do you think?"

"I think we have to figure out better ways to deal with teenagers. We have to send them the message that we don't know everything, that with some love and some trust, they'll do okay. What do you think?"

Ken said, "My wife and I didn't sleep for hours that night. We talked and talked. We hadn't made love in a long time but we made it that night. We didn't even think about it, it just happened. . . . Where'd we get the luck to have a son like John?"

"Ken, you are a lucky man. I don't know where you got it but my advice is, hold on to it. But it wasn't luck when you did what he asked you to do in the end. And, it won't be luck if you keep doing it. Can I put this story in the book? What you and your wife did needs to be told. I don't mean about making love."

"It's okay with me but I have to ask my wife and check with John and Alexis. My days of knowing what's right for everyone, you know, I hope they're coming to an end."

FIVE

DONALD, ROBERT, CURTIS, AND BOB

After one of my recent seminars, attended mostly by school counselors, Donald, a young counselor, sought me out for advice. He had been using my choice theory in his counseling with Robert, a fourteen-year-old African American with whom he'd been able to make a fairly good relationship, but no one else has been able to reach him. In school, he refuses to do any more than enough to get by. He's disruptive in class and a terror at home, where he lives with his grandmother. His mother, the grandmother's only child, has been dead for years; she died from an overdose. He has never known his father, who is serving a life sentence for a murder committed during a botched drug deal. There are no close relatives, and no one besides his grandmother wants anything to do with him. In some way, Donald needs to act as a parent; Robert's grandma is in over her head.

In the large inner-city middle school where Robert is in the eighth grade, he's already involved in some gang activity and is into drinking and smoking pot. His grandmother has been called to school several times because of his behavior, but all she did was beg for advice on how to deal with him at home, where he threatens her if she doesn't give him money. I asked the counselor if Robert has the capability of doing schoolwork. He told me he is quite capable. Even with his lack of interest, he manages to pass his courses and has shown that he can read and write at grade level, maybe above if he'd try.

Because of his huge caseload, Donald has almost no time for Robert, but Robert refuses to take no for an answer when he wants to see Donald. He walks out of class, comes to his office, and just waits. At Donald's request, the principal puts up with this behavior because Donald has convinced him that, if he loses his relationship with Robert, Robert will be in Juvy in a heartbeat. After telling me this dismal but all too common story, Donald looked at me for advice.

I said, "Robert needs someone besides you, someone he can see regularly who's older, responsible, and who will make friends with him without using the external control I just explained in the meeting. Basically, someone he respects who won't tell him what to do. It's his only chance to keep out of custody. He's like a starving person who gets a little sustenance from you but can't get enough to do more than stay alive. Because of you, he knows that food's out there. But he's angry because he can only get enough to keep from starving. Is there anyone you know who could give him more time or get him into a clinic where he could see a counselor once or twice a week to add to what you can give him?"

"No chance. He's seen counselors on and off since he was ten. His grandma got him the appointments, but he was so hostile they felt that they were wasting their time. Robert took their inability to deal with him as a rejection. He's tuned in to testing people's patience, and then when it's found wanting he takes it as a rejection. I have all I can do to sustain the little relationship we have in the time I can give him, and so far I've passed his test, he trusts me. If he can't see me, he settles for my office and my magazines."

Robert represents a large group of seemingly unreachable

young men. What Donald was asking me was the question that I've been asked over and over for the last forty years: What can we do when there seems to be nothing in this situation that anyone can do? There are millions of capable but totally disconnected teenagers in this country like Robert, who are on the fast track for prison or the grave. Without ever having known his father, he is walking the same, all too familiar path his father walked before him. At nineteen, only five years older than he is now, his father was incarcerated for life. Is Robert's life a Greek tragedy, the end foretold, change impossible? I don't think so. This is not a preordained tragedy. But to survive he needs to connect with a responsible person he can care for, someone he believes wants to connect with him.

It seems to Donald that no such person exists but, in my experience, there may be a person Donald has never thought of whom he could tap for this role. I have found such a person on several occasions, not just for young people like Robert but for others from much more affluent backgrounds who were almost as disconnected. This person has served in the form of a kind of peer mentor. When done carefully with some preparation, such intervention has yielded results that were much better than I had any reason to hope for. If Donald was willing to try, as I had, and if he had as good a relationship with Robert as I had with the young people I tried this with, there might be a thread of hope.

I said to Donald, "Do you have a good friend who counsels in a nearby high school?"

He nodded that he did, and I continued, "Would you ask your friend if he knows of a high school boy, sixteen or seventeen years old, who is a good student and is also a very kind, caring young man?"

Donald followed the thread of my thinking and said, "I can do that but what are you driving at?"

"Nothing complicated. I believe a young man like that is your only hope. Robert needs someone besides you to connect with, someone he can respect, who will spend time with him and do nothing else besides try to connect. That means no external control no matter what Robert does or how much he tests. It may be easier for a high school student to see him without external control than it would be for you. You'd have to explain to Robert what you want to do for him, but I don't think there'd be any problem with him understanding why. Besides, there's no one else."

"You think we can teach a high school student enough choice theory to do this?"

"He doesn't have to know that much. He's not going to counsel, just try to connect. Don't make a big deal about knowing choice theory; teach him about the deadly habits and external control and he'll catch on. Kids learn this stuff quicker than adults, a lot quicker than adults with the usual counseling training. They don't have to unlearn a lot of stuff that doesn't work in this situation. Maybe your counselor friend at the high school could send down a small group of them, boys and girls, to do this for a few other students like Robert in your middle school."

"But why would a kid go out of his way to help someone like Robert?"

"Because he's a human being; as long as we don't use a lot of external control on them, most teenagers are loving and caring. You'd explain how badly it's needed. Robert is going to get in big trouble if someone doesn't help us with him. Tell the student you select he's the only one who can do it. Make it a challenge, kids like challenges. They get plenty of bad ones, this is a good one. And you don't have to start with a group, start with one. I thought of a group because I get carried away when I think of all those almost hopeless kids in your school. Robert's bright. For some reason, maybe because he's so intelligent, he's decided to keep up in school. And he can connect. Face it, Donald, he's made enough of a connection with you that you've come to me for help. There's a chance. Why not try? Besides, if the high school student succeeds in connecting with Robert, we'll both benefit. Plus, you've benefited from connecting with Robert, and I'm benefiting from connecting with you. All the streets we work on are two-way."

The conversations in the rest of this chapter are made up. But the thrust of what each is saying is real. Students are acting as peer connectors in many schools. That's what peer mentoring is all about. But what they do is as much or more to connect than to counsel. In the Glasser Quality Schools,* we teach all the students to use choice theory in their lives and to use it when they are having trouble getting along with each other or with their teachers. Students as young as first graders learn it easily and they like learning it. It's also fun to teach. Donald could teach it easily to the high school volunteer. My wife and I did a lot of choice theory teaching when we worked in the Schwab Middle School in Cincinnati in the 1994–95 school year.

Bob, the high school counselor Donald got in touch with, looked around and found Curtis, a sixteen-and-a-half-year-old who seemed to be one of the nicest kids not only in his school but in any school around, just the boy he was looking for. He told him what was needed and Curtis agreed to meet with Donald at the middle school and see if they could work something out. Curtis is big, six-five, weighing close to 200 pounds, a good-natured, good-looking athlete who keeps his grades up. He is obviously an excellent role model for Robert, but when

---

*Glasser Quality Schools are listed in the book *Every Student Can Succeed* (see its appendix A). They are based on choice theory and what I call the *competence-based classroom* in which every student does succeed.

Donald met with him, Curtis was worried about how to get this thing with Robert going. Curtis is not used to failing and he realized this could be a real challenge. After he and Donald shook hands and talked enough for Curtis to understand what was involved, he had some immediate concerns. He said:

"My counselor at the high school explained what I'm supposed to do. Somehow I'm to get tight with this kid, Robert, and become his friend. . . . I know about kids like him, I went to that middle school. We have plenty of Roberts at the high school, but I think they're worse in middle school. Before we go a step further I'd like you to tell me, how am I supposed to do this? The first thing that'll come to his mind is that I'm a narc. I know these kids. I could end up getting killed."

"I was worried about that, too. But when I talked to Robert and told him exactly what's going on, he was interested. I haven't told him who you are because I didn't know, but I knew Bob would find someone. Robert trusts me. I'm the only one around here he does trust. I'll introduce you to him in my office later this week if you're willing."

"What exactly did you tell him? I want to be real clear on that."

"I asked him why he hung around my office so much and he said because I treat him differently from the way everyone else does. I'm not always after him about the way he is and about school. Curtis, that's what I want you to do. Just spend time with him and try to be friends. Don't tell him what he should do or shouldn't do. Tell him a lot about what you do. Like you play football and run track and you're good in school. You like basketball? I think that's what he likes."

"I like it, I'm just better at football and I'm pretty fast for a quarter of a mile. If he likes hoop, I'll be glad to go to the park with him and pick up a game. They know me in the park, I have no trouble getting on the court."

"That'd be a good way to start. Just be careful and don't give him advice. With Robert, it's really more what you don't say than what you do."

"Didn't he ask why I'm willing to spend time with him?"

"Sure he did."

"What'd you tell him?"

"The truth: I'd asked the high school counselor if he could find someone who would treat him just like I do but could spend some more time with him. I'd find a young man he could respect and now that you're here, I think you're the one. He wants to meet you. The rest is up to you, but first I have to teach you a little choice theory. Everything I do is based on that theory. It's totally different from the way everyone is treating Robert. It's not that hard to learn. Just think of how you always want to be treated by everyone and that's choice theory. And don't worry about Robert. He really wants to meet you. If you get along, I'll count on you to spend some time with him."

"How much time? I'm pretty busy."

"I don't know. I'd leave that up to you. He asked me and I told him about an hour a week. Maybe on the weekend."

"An hour a week. That little would help?"

"Half an hour a week would help. It's hard for you to understand. Bob said you have a mother you get along with and a big family. Robert hasn't anyone besides his grandma and they don't get along. The only person he really has right now is me. He sits a lot in my outer office, but I'm so busy I don't have much time to talk with him. No time at all to do anything with him like play basketball."

"Where's his mother, his father?"

"His mother's dead. His father's out of the picture. He lives with his grandma, and she's after him all the time because he doesn't do his schoolwork. She nags him from the time he gets up till the time he goes to bed. It's so bad sometimes he doesn't even come home. I'm real worried about that. If you've got a mother who doesn't nag you all the time, you're lucky."

"She nags but we get along. She's just being a mother. I really don't do anything for her to get that upset about. But look. You didn't ask about my father. You're worried I don't have a father at home, aren't you?"

"I am, I'll admit it. I don't ask that question around here."

"Well, don't worry, I have a father. I've got something not too many kids around here have. He's a great guy; my friends like to hang around when he's home. He's a great man even though my mother acts like she doesn't think so. But it's all an act, they love each other. Bob knows about him, he should have told you. He's a schoolteacher, you'd like him. I told my dad about getting together with you and he told me to do it. If the dude and I get along, he wants to meet him, too."

Then Donald taught Curtis what's written in the first two chapters of this book, about the basic needs and how we all need love and we all need power. Donald explained to Curtis, "When we have love from a mother and father like you have, we don't pay much attention to our need for power. That's why you're so easygoing. But when a kid like Robert doesn't have love from anyone, power's all that's on his mind. That's why he's so angry all the time. That's why there're so many angry kids in this school."

Curtis first met with Robert in Donald's office and they seemed to get along. When they talked about what to do together, they both agreed they liked basketball so Curtis picked up Robert on Saturday morning and they headed straight to the park to get into some half-court, two-on-two. They played hard for almost three hours. Then they sat for a while, ate a good lunch that

Curtis's mother had packed, and talked. Even though he'd had a real good time, Robert still asked, "I don't get it. Okay, I had a good time but why are you doing this? What's in it for you?"

"I'm not sure myself, but I had a good time, too. What I want to know is why aren't you on the school basketball team? You're almost as tall as I am."

"Don't give me that 'I'm not sure' shit. Why are you doing this?"

"Okay, I agreed to do this as long as I could always tell you the truth. And I just did. I did have a good time and I do wonder why you're not out for basketball. But you know what happened. It's just like Donald told you. My high school counselor, Bob, and Donald are friends. Donald called him and said he was worried about you. You were so angry all the time, you were about to get into some big trouble and maybe throw your life away. Donald didn't have enough time but he thought that maybe someone like me would have the time so he called Bob. Bob asked me and here I am. I could see why you liked Donald when we met. That's when I said to myself, I'd like to get to know you and I'm glad I have. Do you like Donald?"

"I do like him. But I never told him I needed a baby-sitter or whatever you think you're doing. I'm a little pissed. I think he's stuck his nose too far into my business."

"We played a little hoop and we had a good time. What's bugging you?"

"The whole fucking world's bugging me. The school, my idiot grandmother, my dead druggie mother, a father in jail that I don't know and I'll never know. All the stupid shit we have to learn and the low grades the teachers give me to make sure I can't play basketball. . . . And in my whole life no one's ever packed me a lunch like we just ate."

After that explosion there was silence. Neither spoke. Then

Curtis said very slowly and carefully, "Is this it? We got together, we had a good time. We ate a good lunch. We're having a good talk and all I am is a baby-sitter so you don't want to see me anymore?"

After he said that, he stopped talking. They just sat and looked at each other. Then Robert started to cry and choked out, "No, I don't. Not if you feel sorry for me."

"I do feel sorry for you. But I feel sorrier for your grandma, for Donald, for all the teachers who have to put up with your shit. And fucking sorry for the basketball coach at your school. If he'd seen how you played today, he'd shit a brick."

"So now you're pissed at me?"

"No, not at all. You're the one that's pissed. There's nothing you can say that'll even come close to making me mad at you. My dad's a schoolteacher. He teaches at a high school not far from this park. I've told him about you. He wants to meet you. Why don't we go see him?"

Do you think I played Curtis as too perfect? Do you think that kids like Curtis don't exist in ghetto schools? I can tell from experience that they do. They are the strength of those schools and I think we shouldn't hesitate to call on them to help. But this is enough. I won't take it further because I see it ending happily and stories like this are not supposed to end happily. But sometimes they do. Young men like Curtis can do more for kids like Robert than the best counselors in the world. And do it quicker and with more lasting effects.

We have trouble with teenagers like Robert because, even though in our hearts we know that external control doesn't work, we still use it because most of us don't know that there's anything better to replace it with. The Glasser Quality Schools I work with have given it up. They use choice theory and they're different. They have the guts to try something beside the seven deadly habits and it works. If Robert is willing to connect with Curtis, he can save his life. Donald and Bob should get credit for doing what they did because there is little else that will work. Robert connects with a positive person or there's no hope.

SIX

ROGER, SUSAN, AND TERI

If professional counseling is affordable, there are times when it may be the best approach for dealing with an unhappy teen, especially when her parents are wedded to external control. I recognized that Roger and Susan were such parents when they came to see me about Teri. But I also need to say that not all professional counseling is the same. I practice a method that I created in 1965 called reality therapy, and it is now taught all over the world. I updated the original reality therapy to include choice theory in 2001. What I teach and practice today is a great improvement over what I created thirty-five years ago.

The counseling I will do with Teri is clearly described in my recent book, *Counseling with Choice Theory: The New Reality Therapy.** In it, the choice theory I explained in chapter 1 has been completely integrated into the way I now counsel. As I work with Teri, it will be easy for you to follow what I do because I will take the time to explain it as I proceed. I don't expect any parent to be a professional counselor, but from my explanation of what I'm doing, you will recognize how you

---

*William Glasser, *Counseling with Choice Theory: The New Reality Therapy* (New York: HarperCollins, 2001).

might use the choice theory approach in dealing with a teenage child.

If you want your teenager counseled the way I counsel, you can use what I explain here to question prospective counselors and compare what they tell you they do with what I did with Teri. For more details, I strongly suggest you read the book *Counseling with Choice Theory.*

Roger and Susan were an attractive, intelligent, fortyish couple who were terribly worried because their sixteen-year-old daughter, Teri, was so difficult compared with her twenty-two-year-old sister, Aileen. From the start, they both made it clear to me that Aileen was perfect in every way—looks, personality, and accomplishments—and they proudly supported everything they said with pictures. Aileen was tall, slender, and beautiful; Teri looked short, dumpy, and unattractive. Aileen, after graduating college early with honors, had been hired to enter training as a production assistant at a major television network. Teri was having trouble passing her high school courses.

Aileen was upbeat, optimistic, and the center of a circle of equally accomplished, attractive girlfriends. In her parents' opinion, Teri suffered mostly from depression, but recently she'd been experiencing severe, almost uncontrollable bouts of anger. Unlike her sister, Teri hung around almost exclusively with two girls who were photocopies of herself. Neither she nor her girlfriends seemed to have the slightest interest in doing anything positive for themselves.

As Roger and Susan went on and on in this vein, it was obvious that, no matter how much they protested they'd come to me for help, they saw themselves stuck with a loser kid and didn't know what to do with her. Very quickly it became obvious to me that they couldn't help Teri, and it was doubtful I could very quickly teach them as much as I was able to teach some of the other parents in this book. They made it clear to me they could afford my help and with a few mentions of "Don't worry about what it costs," sent the message, We're counting on you to take Teri off our hands.

I asked them, "Do you think Teri would be willing to see a counselor?"

Roger said, "We've already talked it over with her and she said she would."

I said, "I'm surprised you waited this long. Has she been seen by anyone else?"

Susan answered, "She's been seeing a psychiatrist her pediatrician recommended but Teri doesn't like her. When we talked to her therapist, she seemed very pessimistic about Teri. She really doesn't counsel that much; mostly she depends on drugs. She's finally settled on Prozac for Teri and has been upping the doses, all the while asking us if the drug is helping."

Roger added, "Teri seems a little less depressed but she's doing something that has us worried. Once in while she goes into these rages, I mean she just tears up her room. She had an expensive collection of china dolls and she destroyed every one. We heard her screaming and banging in her room but by the time we got there, she'd broken them all and told us she felt much better. We don't understand these outbursts. Could that kind of anger have anything to do with her medication?"

"I'm not an expert on this. I've never prescribed psychiatric drugs, but I've heard and even read some research indicating that the class of drugs that includes Prozac has been associated with sudden rages. If you send her to me, I may advise her to stop taking the medication, but she must cut down on it very slowly. Do you think she'd be willing to do that?"

Susan said, "I don' t think that'll be a problem. She says she feels funny on the medication. She doesn't like it. Can we bring her to see you tomorrow?"

"Could she possibly come herself? I don't think you live too far from this office. She's not a baby, she could easily get here on her own."

Roger asked, "But don't you think Susan should be here with her in case you need to talk to her?"

"No, Teri'll be fine alone. In fact, unless she wants to talk with you about what's going on in our counseling, I think it'd be a good idea for you not to ask her about it. If I need to talk with you, I'll be in touch, but I think I'll have to get to know her better before I'll attempt that."

Teri needs to separate herself from the overwhelming control of parents she probably can't please and, at this stage of the relationship, has made up her mind that, even if she could please them, it's the last thing she'd want to do. When I counsel an adolescent like Teri, the counseling process has little chance of working unless she understands right from the start that I'm not seeing her to please her parents or to try to persuade her to please them. In her struggle with her parents, she's crippled herself enough by the role she's chosen to play. I'm also sure she blames them for her inadequacy even though in her struggle for their love, she's chosen to adopt the one behavior, rage, that won't get it.

What she needs to learn in the counseling is that there is no payoff for her in blaming them. Her only chance is to learn to behave adequately regardless of what they do. The more she is able to feel adequate, the more I will be able to help her, but she's been mired in what she's been choosing to do for a long time and won't give it up easily. But if I can help her to make some better choices, she will be on her way to becoming a new Teri, which is actually what her parents want me to help her become.

The new Teri I will try to help her become may not be the

new Teri her parents envision. What they want is for her to be like her sister, who has chosen the opposite route to deal with their control. It will be interesting to see how Roger and Susan deal with a new, more confident Teri if I can help her get to that point. Based on experience, my guess is that one parent will handle it better than the other. Still, I may be overly optimistic that I can help her move toward more competence.

I think you will easily see what I'm trying to do. I'll have to convince her that I'm unlike any adult she has dealt with in recent years and, in doing so, render her inadequate behavior totally unnecessary as she deals with me. I have to start out that way, sort of take her by surprise and hope that she rises to my challenge. I'll give her permission to be more adequate with me. I won't expect her to act with me the way she's been acting with her parents, teachers, or other adults in her life. In short, as quickly as I can, I'll connect with her and create a new, noncontrolling relationship through which she can grow. What you will see me do is give her a chance to make a lot of new, more effective choices. Whether or not I help her depends on my skill as a therapist.

Curiosity is a great motivator. Teri got to my office on her own. When she came in, she seemed almost surprised to have come by herself. But I was surprised, too. From the way her parents had talked and from the pictures they brought with them, pictures that were more of Aileen than Teri, I expected a fat, little ugly duckling. But while she was overweight, it was moderate and she was at least five-four. There was nothing wrong with her looks as far as I could see. It was the way she dressed, the way she'd made up her face, and the hairdo she'd chosen that seemed to be so wrong for her face and figure. There was no doubt in my mind she was making a concerted effort to look different from anything her parents wanted her to look like and had become almost a caricature in the other direction.

I was a long way from talking about her looks or weight. If she becomes less obsessed with being what they don't want, I thought, she should be perfectly capable of doing this on her own. If I can persuade her to become adequate enough to be more of her own person, she'll do fine. It'll be much easier and more satisfying than what she's doing now. She just has to learn that what she does is for herself, not for them or against them.

It only took a moment for all the theorizing I've written above to flash through my mind. Now I had to begin by helping her to relax and get comfortable in my office. To do that, I had to come across as someone much different from who she expected me to be.

I started in by saying, "Teri, I was looking forward to meeting you. I'm glad you're here. I wonder, could you tell me what you've been thinking about since your parents asked you to come to see me?"

For the last few years, I doubt if any adult has looked forward to meeting with Teri. And certainly no adult she's respected has asked what's on her mind. In telling her I'm glad she's here and asking what's on her mind, I'm hoping to find out whether she'll accept me as someone trying to help or reject me as just another counselor she doesn't need. I'm not looking for miracles. All I'm hoping for today is something better than a total rejection.

"I'm only here because my parents wanted me to come. There's nothing wrong with me. Believe me, they're the ones who need help."

Good: not positive, but not that negative, either.

"They've already seen me but I didn't think there was anything I could do to help them even if they did want help, which they don't. But after we talked, I did ask to see you. But believe me, just because you and your parents can't get along, doesn't mean there's something wrong with you. Most of the people who come to see me have nothing wrong with them. What's wrong is that, like you and your parents, they can't get along with the people they live with. I wanted to see you to find out if I can help you. If I think I can, I won't need them. You're not a child, there's a lot you can figure out for yourself. Starting right now, what we talk about here is between you and me. I have no intention of sharing what we say with anyone."

"Whatever, I'd be happy if you like never saw them."

"But it would help me if you'd tell me why you've been seeing a psychiatrist for a while."

"They think I need to change but I'm fine. They're the ones who ought to see that pill pusher they sent me to. I totally know what they told you about me. They told you the same thing they tell anybody who'll listen to them. I'll bet they gave you an earful about my sister. They did, didn't they?"

"A double earful. What about her? I have a hunch you don't see her quite as perfect as they do, but do you get along?"

"That's what bothered me so much about the shrink they sent me to. She wanted to blame all my troubles on my sister. She kept telling me I must hate her because, you know, she's Miss Perfect and I'm the family toad. But I don't hate her; I love her, she's good to me. She keeps telling me I shouldn't pay that much attention to our weirdo parents. I think she's worse off than I am. She just keeps trying and trying to please them and even Miss Perfect can't really do it. There is no pleasing them. I feel sorry for her. At least I don't kill myself trying like she does. I know I'll never please them."

Okay, we're off to a good start, and my hunch about her sister has given me a little credibility. She's talking easily and sensibly to me and I don't think I'll have any trouble talking to her about what's really important: her unhappiness.

"You say you've given up on trying to please them. I think that's a good idea, unless they change and start to make an effort to please you. If you do all the pleasing, you're admitting they have control over you. How much control do your parents really have over you?"

Control is the real issue with Teri, as it is with most teenagers. Adults think that they should have the right to boss their kids around no matter what they do, and teens like Teri fight back. It's the power struggle that's so destructive to the teen-parent relationship. Once they start fighting, they both lose, as have all the teens and their parents in this book except maybe John.

She answered my question by saying, "Not as much as they think they have. But they never give up trying. We fight over everything."

"Look, if it's okay with you, I'd like to stop talking about what your parents want for you and start talking about what you want for yourself. You're sixteen. In two years you'll be old enough to leave home and you might decide to do it. Or your parents could move away to a place you don't want to go. It happens all the time. It's time to start thinking about what you want for yourself."

It's not very likely that she'll soon separate from her parents. But what's important in the counseling is that I do all I can to separate myself from her parents. It'll be hard to help her if she associates anything I say with them.

"You don't want to hear about how they treat me? Like nothing I've done has ever pleased them. They're horrible parents. I can't believe you don't even want to know what they've put me through."

She's trying to keep me connected with them but I'll try to resist by saying, "No, I don't, because I can't change anything they've ever done. And you can't either. You've been through it all and you're still talking good sense. I want to help you to take a look at what your life could be like if you'd stop being unhappy about what goes on at home. You are unhappy, aren't you?"

"Whatever. . . . Okay, I'm unhappy. I've been unhappy for a long time. But you don't understand, like it's not my fault."

Based on choice theory, I believe that the only person's behavior we can control is our own. Blaming or finding fault is a deadly habit. She can't control her parents; blaming them is worthless. She can only control what she does.

To teach her that, I begin by saying, "If you're unhappy, what difference does it make whose fault it is? Suppose I agree with you, that it's not your fault? You'll feel a little better for a minute or two but my agreeing doesn't really change anything. Suppose you missed lunch today and now you're hungry. Are you going to be any less hungry because you forgot your lunch or because someone stole it? Your stomach doesn't care whose fault it is."

"If someone stole it, I'd be angry."

"I'm sure you would. But you'd still be hungry. Angry or not, if you want to eat, you'd still have to figure out how to get food. No matter what happened, your lunch is gone. You can never go back and eat it. You can waste a lot of time being angry at your parents, but do you think being angry at them or fighting with them or breaking all your dolls will change them?"

"They told you about that?"

"Of course they did. They were happy to tell me. It proved you need the help, not them."

I use logic and analogies when I counsel. It helps people to see things they don't want to see.

"Are you trying to tell me that I should just take all their crap without putting up a fight?"

Here I have to make the point that I'm not like her parents or her teachers by saying, "I'm not ever going to tell you that you should do anything. If you're angry and you want to stay angry, that's your choice. But I also may suggest that there may be other ways to deal with your parents besides being angry. Teri, what you choose to do is up to you. But I wonder, do you see yourself as an angry young woman?"

"Yeah, whatever."

I've just barely introduced the idea of choosing. It really hasn't registered yet but, at least, it's out on the table. Now, I'll try to link her anger with unhappiness by saying, "Do you think it's possible to be happy when you're angry? I see a lot of angry people and believe me, they're not happy. It's unhappiness I worry about when I counsel, and you've told me you're unhappy."

I don't want to dwell on this point but she is listening and she'll think about it. I'll go on and ask, "Teri, do you have a few close friends?"

"Yeah. There are three of us. We hang out together. Why?"

"Good, without friends it's almost impossible to be happy. If you've got two good friends, you're lucky. Have you ever thought of why you're friends with these girls? Why you like being with them?"

"I don't know. I guess it's because, you know, they accept me. They're not like adults who're always telling me what I should be doing."

"That's been my experience. Friends accept you as you are. They're a lot different from parents and teachers. Are your friends angry like you are? For instance, do you talk a lot about people you don't like when you get together?"

"Yeah. Mostly we bitch about our parents. But it's stupid, isn't it? Like you just said, we can't change them and they can't change us. You're the psychiatrist. Why do we bother so much about our parents when they'll never change?"

"Because they're trying to control you, and talking about them is a way you defend yourselves. You're in a war you can't win and they can't win, so all of you keep fighting and complaining. I'll bet your parents talk a lot about you, too."

"They do, like right in front of me. It happens all the time."

"If it's stupid to keep fighting when no one's winning, why don't you just stop?"

"Why don't they just stop?"

"Can you stop fighting?"

"No, 'cause I'd lose. No one wants to lose. We have a cool history teacher who's teaching us about Vietnam. Nobody wanted to lose, so you know, they kept killing each other."

"But it did end. Finally, we pulled out. Do you think you could pull out of this war with your parents?"

"You mean give in to them?"

"No, I mean just tell them or maybe just tell yourself, 'Since neither of us is ever going to win, I'm going to stop fighting. I haven't done what you want me to do for a long time, so you can keep after me if you want to but I'm not going to fight with you anymore.' What do you think they'd say?"

"Nothing, because I'd never say that to them in a million years. I don't talk to them and they don't talk to me. I mean we say pass the salt or I need lunch money. But talk, I mean talk like we're talking now. Talk like you just suggested I talk with them. It'll never happen."

"Do you like to talk the way we're talking now?"

"It's okay but in the end nothing's gonna happen. It's just talk."

"I'm not sure of that. I think this talk could lead to you doing something about what's going on at home. Do you want to do something?"

"No, I want my parents to do something."

"I think they may if you stop the fighting and do something different from what you've been doing."

"Something I guess you're going to suggest?"

"I'm hoping it'll be something you might figure out on your own if we talk some more. I think it'll help if you can tell me what you want. Like what it would be like if you won a battle in this war. Don't worry if what you want seems impossible. Start with one thing. Any one thing you want that, if you had it, you'd be happier."

"Okay, I'll tell you what I want. I want to stop hearing about school. Not one word about school or grades or what will happen if I don't get good grades. After every report card I get grounded for a month. I hate school, I really hate it. When those kids shot up that high school in Colorado, I can totally understand why they did it."

"Did you always hate school?"

"No, I loved elementary school. I had good teachers. I loved the reading and writing. I don't even like to read anymore. I even liked math. If they'd figure out a high school like that grade school, I'd go in a minute."

"But then what happened?"

"It started in middle school and it's been the same stuff ever since, and it's all boring."

"Do you plan to work hard enough to graduate?"

"Yeah, I'll graduate. If you pass a couple of tests and hand in a few papers, they pass you. I learned more than enough in elementary school to graduate from the crummy high school I go to. I may even go to the community college. The kids who go there say it's cool. But I've got to survive that prison I'm in for two more years. All I hear from my parents is the university and how well Aileen did there. You asked me what I want. I just don't want to hear another word about school."

"Okay, tell me: Who pays more attention to your parents, you or your sister?"

"She does. She sucks up to them all the time. They just bought her a new Mustang. They give her anything she wants. It's nauseating. But like I said, she's nice to me. I love her. If it weren't for her I think I'd have run away from home. She keeps telling me to suck up and I could, like, have all the stuff she has. I guess you're gonna tell me to start sucking up, too. I could feel it coming when you asked that question about my sister."

"Excuse me if I don't agree with you. You may not suck up but I think you pay more attention to your parents than she does. Much more."

"No way. What do you mean?"

"I think your sister's figured out that because someone tells her to do something, even if they think it's for them, it might actually be good for her, too. I saw pictures of your sister. Her face looked pretty good. Your face doesn't look as good as her face. But I'll also bet that if you and she were here with me and you went into the washroom and scrubbed your faces, hers wouldn't look any better than yours. You've seen it, is her scrubbed face that much prettier than your scrubbed face?"

"She's prettier."

"A lot prettier?"

"No, not a lot prettier. But I don't want to look like her. She looks like my mother wants her to look."

"But that's what I'm trying to tell you. Everything you do including your makeup shouts 'you can't control me' at your parents. Their control is more on your mind than on your sister's. By all your fighting with them, you've actually encouraged them to examine your life. They buy Aileen a car and they don't look deeply into where she drives it. If you don't believe me, ask her. You've spent years resisting your parents. So much so, you don't even have a life."

When I said that, Teri looked directly at me for the first time. She didn't say anything. I knew I'd gotten through. Finally she said, "So what do I do?"

"If I were you, I'd talk it over with your sister. She loves you. See if she agrees."

"She'll agree. She's been telling me the same thing forever. But you know, girls don't listen to their sisters. I'm not going to give in to her, either."

"If you do what I've just explained, you won't be giving in to anyone but yourself. But if you decide to do anything they want you to do, don't tell them we talked about this. They might say something like, 'See, we knew you needed a psychiatrist,' and try to take credit for what you may be doing. Believe me, if you start to act on what I've just explained and it works, it'll be because of what you do, not the little bit I just explained. My job's the easy part. You've got the hard part and I want to help you do it. Don't do anything for a week but talk to your sister and figure out a few things you could do differently. Keep in mind that because your parents want you to do something doesn't automatically make it bad for you. Resist the university, you're not ready for that. But don't resist changing your makeup, hairdo, or how you dress just because the change may please your parents. When we get together next week, we can talk more about this."

We'll hear more from Teri in a later chapter, but if you are a parent, I think you might learn something here. Don't push your kids to do things they don't want to do. Talk to them about doing things that are good for them, not for you. If you start in that way when they're small, you can avoid a lot of the trouble Roger and Susan have had. And as I said before, if she changes as I've suggested, it will be interesting to see how her parents deal with it. Remember, external control people don't give up external control easily even if it's to their benefit to do so.

SEVEN

JACKIE AND JOAN

There are times when a teenager's behavior is so difficult to deal with that a devoted parent has to accept there is nothing she can do. Such a teen was Jackie; such a parent was Joan. I only met Jackie twice but I guided Joan through a very difficult time with her. Joan brought Jackie to my office because she was desperate to learn what she should do. It didn't take me long to understand her desperation. She had seen some other counselors with Jackie, but after a few sessions none of them would see her anymore.

Jackie was slim, attractive, and neatly, though funkily, dressed in the avant-garde style of the time. But except for her perpetual scowl, there was nothing about her appearance that would give any indication of her behavior. Although I usually see teenage girls by themselves, as soon as Jackie opened up her mouth I was relieved that Joan was there. She was without a doubt the most repulsive teenage girl I had ever met in my practice and since then I've never met her equal.

Joan was quite attractive, tastefully dressed, and perceptively soft-spoken. As soon as Jackie opened her mouth, I could see that Joan was embarrassed at having had to bring her into my office. I sympathized. I was embarrassed for Joan's discomfort at having to bring such a girl anywhere.

Joan and I had talked for about ten minutes on the phone,

so, in a sense, we were acquainted and she tried to introduce me to Jackie. But almost immediately, before her mother could open her mouth, Jackie said, "The fucking bitch dragged me in here. So I guess you'll have to listen to what the bitch has to say."

In my years of practice, I've seen a lot of nasty teenagers, boys and girls, but *nasty* was not the adjective for Jackie. I was repelled by her. I'd never heard a child refer to her mother to her face as Jackie just had. It wasn't only the words; it was the tone of her voice, the scowl on her face, and the implication, This is the way I am and the way I intend to be, and you and no one else are going to do a thing about it. I couldn't hide my shock and I could see that it made her happy. She'd wanted to shock me.

Joan just sat there and gave me an imploring look that said, I desperately need help—I know how you feel and I'm embarrassed to bring her here but please see her. I got the feeling she felt she didn't have the right to bring someone like Jackie into my office. I was ashamed that I was unable to hide my shock. I gathered myself together and decided to take Jackie at her word, so I looked at both of them and said, "I'd like to hear what you have to say. Actually, I'd like to hear what you both have to say."

Joan said, "My husband and I don't know what to do with her. You heard what she just called me and I could see your shock. But I really don't hear it anymore. She's been referring to me like that since she was fourteen; she's almost sixteen now. She talks like that or worse to everyone, especially school bus drivers and teachers when she goes to school, which is not very often. She's constantly being suspended. She even verbally attacks strangers in restaurants, sometimes passersby on the streets. The thing is it's totally unpredictable. Once in a while she has a normal day but it's getting worse. Now she's really after us because she wants a car but she hasn't even got a learner's permit because she won't study for the test."

"I'll pass that fucking test so you better get me a car. If you don't, I'm going to burn down your goddamn house."

Joan paid no attention to the threat and went on, "Now things are getting out of hand. She's become involved with the police on almost a weekly basis. They tell us to keep her home but how can we? She just walks out and goes to the mall; it's only a few blocks away. That's where she hangs out with the few friends she manages to keep. Her friends don't make trouble but they encourage her. Her new trick is to scream obscenities at people going the other way on the escalator, and her friends all love it because the people can't get at her. There's a movie complex at the mall and she used to behave there. But now she's started talking to the screen and getting the whole audience worked up. When they tell her to shut up, she starts in with the audience. That's when the police come. They bring her home and tell us we've got to keep her out of the mall but we can't. They say get her some help but no one will see her. It's her mouth. It's not against the law so they keep bringing her home. She curses them all the way home in the police car. They tell me she needs psychiatric care, so here we are. Nobody wants to be with her except the few kids she tries to hang out with and they're getting tired of her, too. Some of them have had pot on them and they get real nervous when the police come around."

Jackie hadn't said anything. I think she enjoyed hearing her mother describe her exploits. But when her mother stopped talking, she said, "Fuck the police, fuck everybody." Then she looked at me and said quite calmly, "You're a shrink. My mother's got money, she'll pay you. Tell her what to do with me."

I said to Joan, "I'd like to talk with Jackie by myself. Would you wait in the waiting room?"

Almost as if she was propelled by a rocket, Joan shot out of her chair and walked out the door. As soon as she was gone, I said to Jackie, "I think it'd be easier if we talked by ourselves. Is there anything you'd like to tell me?"

Truthfully, I didn't know what to say. But I thought I'd give her mother a little rest from her. As long as her mother was in the room, she'd show off.

Jackie looked at me for a few minutes as if she were a scientist looking at a bacterium under a microscope. Then she said, "I've really been pretty good today. I came quietly and just sat here while the bitch told you about me. It's all true. I'm really a lot worse than she said. What the fuck can you do for me? I don't even know what I want for myself. I feel sorry for the fucking bitch, I'd hate to have a child like me. She doesn't know what to do. I think if they'll get me a car so I'm not stuck home all the time, I'll be okay. I know what you can do for me, tell them to buy me a car."

I didn't answer that request. The idea of having her behind the wheel of a car was beyond my ability to conceive. It was almost as bad as if she'd asked me to tell them to get her a gun. Since my focus is on relationships, I ventured, "Is there anything or anyone you like?"

I was surprised by what she said. "There's two cops, one a man and the other a woman, they work together. They're young and they've picked me up a few times and taken me home. I kind of like them. I've asked if I could ride around in the car with them, I told them I'd be good. They're not like the other cops. When I talked like this to them they didn't act like I was anyone they had to shut up, so I stopped talking that way. They were nice. They just drove me home very slowly so I could get a little time in the car and I calmed down. They didn't seem to hate me. That's when I asked if I could drive around with them. They parked with me in front of my house for a while and told me I needed some help. I liked being with them in that car. I think I'd like to be a cop someday."

The rest of the time, about half an hour, we managed to talk a little. She told me in detail about all the havoc she wreaked whenever she went anywhere. She told me the only time she was quiet was when she listened to her rock music at home. I just listened. It's not that she was friendly but I didn't feel any hostility from her. She was the most disconnected human being I'd ever met. It was almost as if her unhappiness had led her to a fork in the road and unlike most unhappy people who gravitate toward getting more love and belonging, Jackie had chosen the other road. She chose her destructive behavior even if it was disconnecting in order to gain more power and freedom. But with the police now involved, the control she thought she was gaining was only an illusion. She was much closer to big trouble than she realized. When we were finished with the session, her mother came back into the office and to my surprise Jackie gave her a smile and said to me, "Don't blame her, it's not her fault."

They made an appointment for the next week. She came in with her mother again but her mother stayed in the waiting room. She was quieter and didn't curse or call her mother a bad name. What I guess was going on was that she didn't sense any desire on my part to control her. I was a little like the two police officers. When we talked, it was as if I was with a young woman who had no clue what to do with her life as a teenager because nothing she had experienced so far satisfied her.

She rambled on for about half an hour and I just listened. I noted that this time she didn't bad-mouth her parents. Somehow, maybe because we made a small connection, she must have realized she needed them. But she had abusive words for her younger brother, grandmother, everyone in her school, people who attended the movies; basically, she had not a kind word for any member of the human race.

I decided to venture a question: "Jackie, does it ever occur to you that when you have trouble getting along with people, it's you, not they, who need to change?"

She looked at me and said, "Of course that's occurred to me. That's why I'm here talking to you. If you think there's something wrong with me, here I am, fix me."

I said, "Okay, let me ask you a question that I don't think anyone has ever asked you. Have you ever forgotten about yourself for a moment and tried to help another person you're close to like your parents or your brother?"

"Help them? Why? My parents' job is to help me and my brother, he's plenty fucked up, too. What they ought to do is buy me a car so I'm not stuck at home all the time."

"I mean help them by paying attention in school so they don't worry about your education."

"Forget it. I hate school, I hate teachers, and I hate homework."

"Do you hate it because you can't do the work?"

"You think I'm stupid?"

"You seem pretty smart to me. But I've met a lot of girls who seem smart to me who have a lot of trouble doing schoolwork. A few of them couldn't even read."

"I can read and write. I was good in elementary school. I didn't like it but it was a lot better than high school. What I hate are people telling me what to do or what not to do. Fuck 'em. If I want to talk in the movies, they can't stop me. You start telling me what to do and I'll never come back."

Basically this was pretty much the way the conversation went. She spent her time waving a red flag at the world and then resented it because the world got on her case. Still, when she left I was satisfied. We'd managed a conversation with very little profanity, none directed at me. I've dealt with teens who were sensitive to external control but Jackie was off the scale.

Her mother called me in a few days to say that Jackie seemed to like me and was willing to come back for another appointment, but she'd been picked up by the police and from what her mother could find out there'd been a real fight with two male police officers who were taking her home from the mall. Jackie claimed she had attacked them because they groped her body while they were trying to get her into the car. She claimed her attack was self-defense. Not only had they groped her, she said, they'd made sexual remarks while they were doing it.

Joan told me she'd done a pretty good job on them with her fingernails and kicks in the groin. They took her to juvenile hall and charged her with resisting arrest and assaulting a police officer. Before they got her into the hall, she demanded that she be allowed the one phone call she was entitled to and she called her mother. On the phone she demanded that her mother come right to the booking desk and get her out of there. She told her mother not to come without a lawyer. They'd told her that a lawyer might be able to help her.

Without consulting with anyone Joan told her she wasn't going to come down there yet. She'd have to talk to me and to her lawyer. There would be a preliminary hearing in a few days and she'd be there. Jackie was furious and cursed her but Joan held fast. Whether she knew it or not, she'd followed some of the best advice I've ever been given: If you don't know what to do, do nothing. I couldn't see Joan until the next morning.

By the time I could see her she'd been in touch with the social worker at the juvenile hall, who told her that Jackie's mouth had been uncontrollable to the point where she almost started a riot. She was put into isolation for her own protection. The preliminary hearing was set for the next day, and Joan was told that if she wished, she could bring a lawyer to the hearing.

Joan started in by asking, "What should we do? Last night, with her in the hall, was the most peaceful night at our house in two years. I hate her being there but I dread her coming home even more. I've called our lawyer and he said to talk to you before we did anything. He knows about her. We've been threatened with some legal action before because of her behavior."

I said, "All I can tell you is what I'd do if she were my daughter. I can't see one redeeming feature about her life with you at home. She's got to be the most unhappy young woman I've ever seen and I've seen my share of them."

Joan had read my 1965 book, *Reality Therapy,** in which I described my work in the Ventura School for Girls, a California State correctional facility for girls fifteen to twenty years old. That's why she came to see me. My experience there with the few girls I'd dealt with who were like Jackie had convinced me they needed a custodial situation. They couldn't handle freedom. But custodial doesn't have to be punitive; at the Ventura School, we never were. If she could be put in such a place, she might accept that there was a real world with some real rules. It would be slow but it might happen.

I explained to Joan that girls like Jackie have no idea what to do with themselves if they are free to go to the mall as she was doing. They say they want people to leave them alone, but they go out of their way to make it impossible to be left alone.

I said, "If she winds up in the county treatment center for girls like her, she'll be lucky. They treat the girls well. My take on it is they may accept her into treatment. Bad as she is, it's been mostly with her mouth and she's a first-time offender. Also, they don't often get a girl from an affluent home and they'll be curious. She'll also be kind of a challenge, to show her parents what they can do for a girl like her that no one has yet been able to do. My advice is, if they are willing to put her into that pro-

---

*William Glasser, *Reality Therapy, a New Approach to Psychiatry* (New York: Harper & Row, 1965).

gram for a few months, leave her there. Don't try to get her out or even to fight the charges against her. It's a juvenile offense. She'll have no record. Visit her regularly. Be warm and loving; she didn't bad-mouth you at all in our second session. She needs you but she needs you in a situation where you can be with her but she can't get at you. Visiting her while she is in custody is ideal. Tell her that you're not going to intervene or get her a lawyer. If the court gets her a lawyer, it's fine with you but you are going to let the juvenile justice system handle the whole thing. No matter how she treats you, how she threatens or begs, keep visiting, both you and her father. Call her, write to her, and send a few clothes. She needs to know you care but that you won't do anything else for her. Don't talk about the past or the future with her; stick to the present. Don't make any suggestions as to how she should be treated; leave it all up to them. Only see her at the regular visiting hours but no matter how she treats you see her two or three times a week if they'll let you. But that's all. Always call so she knows you're coming. If she won't see you when you come, send a message saying you'll wait as long as they'll let you and when you leave, tell them to tell her when you'll be back."

"But she's not a criminal, she'll be with criminals. It's her first arrest. Shouldn't we do more?"

"You do what you think is best but keep in mind that last night you had the first peace in two years. If it was peaceful for you, it might soon be peaceful for her. They'll treat her well. Remember, she was peaceful in the police car with the female officer. This is an extension of that."

Then Joan asked me, "What makes her the way she is? It's all so self-defeating."

I explained choice theory to her. It was before I'd written the book but she understood what I was talking about. I then said, "We're all driven by the five basic needs. If we can satisfy them reasonably well, we're happy. If we can't, we're unhappy. It's up to us to satisfy them, and everyone does it differently. Generally, the most difficult need to satisfy is the need for love and belonging because we need someone else, we can't do that by ourselves. But because we live in an external control society and, essentially, all use the deadly habits, most of us have difficulty with our relationships. Then like so many of us, Jackie, as much as anyone I've ever met, disconnects herself from people, especially from the people she needs, like you and her father. Then when she finds herself disconnected, she uses the habits to try to reconnect but disconnects further. It's like starting a fire with gasoline and throwing on more gasoline to put it out. That's what you meant when you said, 'It's all so self-defeating.' "

Joan said, "I see what you mean."

"But it's even worse. If she's unable to satisfy her need for love and belonging, she turns to the two needs, power and freedom, that may seem easier to satisfy but which will further disconnect her if she succeeds in satisfying them. She uses all that violent language for gaining both power and freedom. If she can't find a way to get connected again, she'll stay the same or get worse. That's why it's so important you visit her. She needs you. But you can visit without saying anything controlling, the way you feel you have to do all the time at home. She may blame you for leaving her in there but I think she needs you enough so it won't make that much difference in the final outcome."

"But we always loved her. We did. Why didn't she feel loved?"

"No one can answer that question. All we know is what we see, and that girl's disconnected. It's like an inoculation. For some reason your love didn't take. But it's not too late. If you keep seeing her and don't allow yourselves to be rejected by her, it may take now. Just see her and don't use the habits, and you have a good chance but no guarantees."

"How good a chance?"

"From my experience, better than fifty-fifty."

"I'll take it unless you have a better offer."

"I'll help you. Keep in touch."

Joan and her husband took my advice. Joan came to see me about every two weeks to talk about her progress. At the treatment unit they'd heard about Jackie's mouth and didn't want her. But with no previous record and the judge's recommendation, they decided to take her. The first month the visits were a nightmare. The cursing and threatening were unbelievable. Jackie could not accept that her mother had left her there. I told Joan to tell her it was on my advice, and that helped a little. I believe that when you're dealing with human relationships, always tell the truth, and this was the truth.

The second month Jackie started to change. She had good visits with both her parents and stopped talking about leaving. She began to relate first to the counselor who saw her individually and then to the group, which met daily. In a real about-face she identified with the counselors and started to make an effort to help other kids. She stopped bad-mouthing her parents and even defended them a little, saying, "They had their hands full with me."

By the middle of the third month the staff started talking about sending her home. But she didn't want to go. She was afraid she wouldn't make it in public school: too much external control. When Joan talked to me about this, I agreed. At the Ventura School, we noted that almost none of our girls could make it in public school, especially when the school heard that the girl had been at Ventura. We advised them not even to try. We recommended they get a job if they were sixteen and then go to junior college where, with a little more maturity and much less control, most of them made it. If they weren't academically inclined, they could learn a trade.

Then an opportunity to go to an out-of-state private school came up. Jackie wouldn't be locked up, but the school was in such an isolated place that few students ran away. She stayed there about two years, made friends, did very well in the classes, and got her high school diploma. Now she was almost eighteen years old and still didn't want to come home. Mostly it was because she had gotten romantically involved with a staff person who actually asked her parents if he could marry her.

They got married; she became pregnant and had a baby. The marriage fell apart but she kept the baby, came home, and got an apartment near her parents. She was a very good mother and immediately got involved with her own mother and father. She also had gotten involved in religion at the private school and had totally stopped cursing. After that I lost track of her because her mother stopped seeing me.

I believe that letting Jackie stay in custody when, with their money and influence, they might have gotten her out was crucial to her rehabilitation. By now she is a grown woman but I have no idea what she is doing. My guess is she has remarried. If anything serious had happened, I'm sure I would have heard from her mother. The last time I talked to her mother she told me they were on very good terms. If you had been with me when I met Jackie and her mother and seen what she was and what she has now become, you'd have trouble believing your eyes. The key is that she had parents who both cared and persisted.

I think there are lots of parents who really care but are having trouble with their teens. I believe that the difference between the parents who succeed in overcoming that trouble and the parents who don't is that the former use choice theory. Although not every parent has the luxury of being able to afford a private school as Jackie's parents did, if we could persuade all schools to use choice theory, as I am devoted to trying to do, we wouldn't have as much of a problem with young people as we have.

Again, if you have a child who hates school, I strongly suggest that you read my recent book, *Every Student Can Succeed.*

Although I saw Jackie many years ago, I would respond in essentially the same way I did with her and her parents if I were seeing them today. You may have noticed that I did not use a diagnostic label to describe Jackie, nor would I label her today. I believe that those labels so freely applied now do damage to children, and I never use them. Instead, I use the terms *unhappy* and *disconnected,* as that is what these teens are. The core of what I would do now, and what I would recommend for teenagers like Jackie, is to teach them and their parents the choice theory I describe in this book.

EIGHT

MORE CHOICE THEORY— STARR, SARA, AND ED

When Sara and Ed called me, they told me they were looking for advice on how to deal with Starr, their anorexic fifteen-year-old daughter. They were desperate. She'd been starving herself in front of their eyes for almost a year, all the while insisting she was too fat. She'd been going to a clinic specializing in anorexia recommended by her pediatrician, but they wanted more information on both the disease and how they should treat Starr at home.

I told them I wasn't an expert on the treatment of anorexia and I would not interfere with what the clinic was doing. I explained that my expertise was in teaching parents how to deal with problem teens, and we all agreed that a girl with anorexia was the epitome of a problem teen. I was more than willing to see them but, before they came in, I wanted them to read the first two chapters of this book so they could get a basic understanding of the choice theory I teach to parents.

Besides those chapters, I also included the additional choice theory material that follows and told them that when they finished it, they should call me and I'd see them right away. I will come back to my meeting with them later in the chapter, but now I want to introduce some additional material about choice theory that I believe sheds important light on anorexia and similar teen problems. I think choice theory is especially apropos to this problem because, if we choose all that we do, choosing to starve themselves is probably the most puzzling and self-destructive choice that teenage girls make.

While it is usually called a disease, anorexia is better described as an addiction or an addictive behavior. Unlike what we usually think of as a disease, there is no pathology in the child's brain or anywhere else in her body. Starving yourself doesn't destroy any particular group of cells that would explain anything. Every cell in the anorexic's body begins to break down until life itself is threatened. Also, in contrast to any disease I've ever heard of, in an addiction the cure is obvious. All an alcoholic has to do to be reasonably healthy is to choose to stop drinking. All Starr had to do was choose to eat more food.

To understand Starr's behavior, I have to expand on chapter 2 by explaining another important element of choice theory. To review for a moment, choice theory explains that we choose all we do in an effort to satisfy one or more of five genetic needs: survival, love and belonging, power, freedom, and fun. Starr is obviously not satisfying her need to survive, and I don't think starving herself is much fun. In the spring of 2001, I saw a *Nova* program on KCET, Los Angeles, about anorexia and there wasn't a trace of fun in any of the many anorexics depicted on the screen. Few smiled, none laughed.

Therefore, in some way they must be starving themselves in an attempt to satisfy one or more of the three other needs: love and belonging, power, or freedom. Certainly, the excuse that many of them give to justify their not eating is that it will make them more attractive, closer to fitting the present media ideal of superthin. But for women to want to be very thin to feel more attractive is not a new idea. Seventy years ago, the duchess of Windsor, certainly a woman driven by her desire for power, said, "A woman can never be too rich or too thin."

While refusing to eat may be an attempt on the part of some young women to make themselves more attractive and thus get more love, this was not apparent in the ultrathin young women depicted on the *Nova* program. None of them mentioned attracting anyone with their new body. In some cases the opposite was true. As they passed from thinness to emaciation, it was obvious they were not starving themselves for others. For reasons that I will now try to explain, they were doing it for themselves in an attempt to experience the feeling of power, the goal of every addict I've known.

There may also be some attempt to satisfy their need for freedom in the sense that *It's my body and I'm free to do what I want with it.* But to live with them, as Ed and Sara are living with Starr, is to experience daily their complete resistance to reason. That anorexics continue to choose to starve themselves against all advice from family, friends, and physicians leads me to believe that they, like all addicts, are driven past any sense of reason by their desire to experience more power than they have ever felt before.

The feeling of having more power than ever before is the heart and soul of addiction, so much so that no matter how much power addicts may have, it is never enough. To get that feeling, there is no price that addicts are unwilling to pay. They are willing to harm themselves by staying with their addiction for the chance to gain a sense of power that goes beyond admiration and respect. It even extends to their belief that they have gained so much power that people are now afraid of what they may do. Starr's parents live in fear of her starving herself to death, and their fear is justified. It is well known that 1 or 2 percent of anorexics starve themselves to death each year.

Bodybuilders who risk their lives by taking steroids do so not only to get the muscles they want to display but also to feel the power that they believe makes lesser men envious or fearful of them. A significant percentage of bodybuilders are addicted to their activity. Starr would be on the other side of the coin from this group. She may use laxatives instead of steroids but her dedication to slimness is as strong as theirs is to bulging muscles.

Gambling is one of the strongest addictions of all. No one feels more powerful than a gambler on a winning streak. Starr's parents may fear for her. Gamblers' families fear both for the gamblers and for themselves. No one will resort to more devious or hostile means to get the money to try for another winning streak than a gambler. Much of that money comes from their family and friends.

If the basic problem of all people, barring poverty, incurable disease, and tyranny, is unsatisfying relationships, then I think few anorexics, alcoholics, or other addicts care that much about what happens to the people in their lives who may be affected by what they're doing. These are lonely, disconnected people who in many instances, like the gambler, *use* the people who love them. Most of them are not very good at accepting love or reaching out to give the love that they need to give if they are to connect or reconnect with the important people in their lives.

To be cured of their addiction, they have to make an effort both to give and to accept enough love and belonging to satisfy themselves and to help satisfy someone else. If they can get to the point where they are willing to do this, there can come a time when the addict will say *enough*: I don't need more muscles or more winning streaks. Or Starr would say, *I'm too thin, this is ridiculous*. It's not that all these addicts lack love. Many of them have been given a lot of love. What they seem to lack is the belief that love is what they need; they are so into power that love has taken a backseat.

What drives them to pursue their self-destructive addiction to power in the face of family and friends who love them is partly revealed by a component of choice theory I have yet to explain that I call *our quality world*. True, it does not fully explain addictions. There are elements of addiction that are not yet understood by anyone. But I believe that what I will explain next will be helpful to anyone such as Starr's parents, involved with an addict.

OUR QUALITY WORLD

I believe that our quality world, a small but vital part of what we know, is the core of our life. In it we store the memory of experiences that, at the time, felt very good and best satisfied one or more of our genetic needs. We start to build this knowledge at birth and we keep adding new experiences to it and taking old experiences out of it for the rest of our lives. It is under our complete control. No one except us can put anything into our quality world or take anything out of it.

But as much as it is under our control, many people, and I believe Starr is one of them, find it almost impossible to remove some experiences, no matter how self-destructive, from their quality worlds. Starr, for example, has put the experience of not eating and getting thinner into her quality world. She doesn't want to pay the price of taking it out. For her, that price is too high, she'll lose too much power. The only way to help her is for someone, in her case it could be her parents, to convince her that the price of taking the idea of not eating and getting thinner out of her quality world is worth paying.

That price is to accept that there are ways to feel good that are as satisfying and may be even better for her than the addictive experience. The price drug addicts have to pay is getting along without the alcohol or other drug. The price bodybuilders have to pay is getting along with muscles they can build without steroids. Gamblers have to be willing to accept that there are other ways to feel good without gambling.

Starr would seem to have an easier price to pay; all she has to do is start eating more food. But it isn't. It's as high a price for her as for any addict, because the addiction experience is firmly embedded into her quality world. Some anorexics, like some drug addicts, would rather die than take it out, and it is impossible to tell who these zealots are in advance. The only way to know this is to try to help them and to see what happens. In the case of Starr, even if what I will suggest her parents do does not work, it is well worth trying. It can do no harm.

For all of us, certainly including Starr, *our quality world is built from the way we picture or perceive three very common but different kinds of life experiences.* The first and most important is how Starr has interacted with some of the *important people* in her life, in her case most likely her parents. The second is how she interacts with *things* in her life, for example, her food and her bathroom scale. The third are the *systems of belief* that drive her behavior. If she were a nun, it would be her belief in God. In her case, it is her seemingly unshakable belief that she should weigh less than whatever is registered on her scale or be thinner than whatever she sees in the mirror. To eat is to lose power.

The pictures in our quality world are so important and so difficult to change because they are built on very good feelings: either how we felt in the past, how we feel now, or how we anticipate we will feel in the future. No matter how we choose to live our lives, those choices are governed by our wanting to feel as good as we can now or in the future. Or our wanting to avoid as much pain as we can now and in the future. Many of us are willing to suffer a great deal of pain now if we believe that in the future there will be a big payoff in pleasure for what we are doing. One example of this is seen in young people who are training for the Olympics.

We put pictures of the people, the things, and the systems of belief we have enjoyed in the past, enjoy now, or hope to enjoy in the future into our quality world. Under most circumstances, those pictures will stay there until we find something else in that category that feels better. For example, wine connoisseurs are continually adding and, once in a while, subtracting wines from their quality world. After a divorce, husbands and wives may take their exes out of their quality worlds and put a new love into it. But some don't. Some may carry the torch for an ex the rest of their lives and suffer because they do, all the while believing it would feel worse to take the ex out.

The key criterion for keeping a picture in our quality world, no matter how difficult it may be to satisfy or how self-destructive it may be, is how good the experience felt when we chose to put it in. We don't know how good Starr's picture of herself, as thinner than she is now, feels in her quality world. It may feel very good. But we do know that it felt good enough early in her weight-loss effort so that she cannot accept taking it out now even if it doesn't actually feel that good. She'll keep it in and continue to starve herself in the hope that a new good feeling will trump all the others. Don't underestimate the strength of this hope.

Alcoholics who are dying of cirrhosis of the liver and smokers dying of emphysema have told me that the picture of enjoyable drinking and smoking is still very much in their quality worlds. Of course, these people don't know anything more about the concept of the quality world than most readers do. I am explaining it here because it is something that people like Ed and Sara need to know. Otherwise, Starr's behavior would be inexplicable.

The first person most of us put into our quality worlds is our mother. When we were born we had the ability not only to feel but to recognize the difference between feeling good and feeling bad, and to learn from this difference. At birth, we didn't know about feeling good or bad but we soon learned it. Very quickly, we became aware that something important in our life was going on when we felt bad and that something soon led us to feeling better. In a very short time we recognized that this good feeling had to do with the combination of our mother, food, and love. All this felt so good that we put our mother into our quality world, and most of us have kept her there ever since, many of us even after she passed away.

After our mother we put a group of other people, relatives and friends, into our quality world because we could count on them to help us find love and many other need-satisfying things that feel very good. Our quality world is the core of our lives because it continually points us in the direction of feeling good either now or later.

Unfortunately, driven by that thinner picture in her quality world, Starr won't consider anything different from what she is doing. The bodybuilder will take steroids, the gambler will continue to gamble, the alcoholic will drink.

For reasons we don't know and may never know, research has shown, Starr has a picture of herself in her quality world thinner than whatever she sees in the mirror. If she continues to keep that picture she will starve herself to death and feel ecstatic in the process, because for her, starving feels good, not bad.

However, I don't believe that she wants to starve herself to death. She'd lose the ecstasy if that happened.

We may never know the exact reason for her picture but, as I have been saying all along, I firmly believe it has to do with satisfying her need for power. People have starved themselves for power throughout history. Mahatma Gandhi starved himself to try to gain freedom for India. Hunger strikes, especially in Northern Irish prisons, are well-known events. But Starr isn't on a hunger strike. She's starving herself because it feels good.

Think of our quality world as the place where we live. One day we meet a very friendly tiger. He's fun to pal around with; people pay attention to him and he asks, "We're having so much fun. Why don't you let me move in with you?" At the time, it seems to be such a good idea, you agree. For a while, he's a great companion. People are amazed you've managed to snare such a sleek, beautiful, and powerful companion. Once he moves in, he turns out to have some bad habits, but you keep remembering all the good things about him so you let him stay.

You spend your time desperately trying to recapture the pleasure you had when you took him in but it's harder and harder to do. You think about throwing him out but, since everyone sees you're still with him and you don't complain about him, it's hard for you to admit to anyone, even to yourself, that taking him in was a bad idea. Also, whatever faults he may have, to you he's still powerful and protective.

It will take a long time but you may finally get rid of him. You're older now and you can stand on your own two feet without him. But you may not. A few people may decide they don't want to live without his power. Starr may be one of them. One day when you're not looking, he starts to eat you up. Just before he swallows you, you ask why and he tells you, *That's what tigers do.* Many of the hunger strikers died and accomplished nothing.

I believe that as Starr entered adolescence, the idea of being modishly thin appealed to her, as it does to a majority of teens who come from well-off parents. She started to lose weight and it felt very good. But then Starr deviated from the pattern of most teenage girls who begin to lose weight. She began to realize that she didn't have control over her parents, friends, or her teachers in school. She also didn't have that much control over what she looked like or how tall she was.

She became more and more intrigued with the fact that she had control over what she weighed. No one, parents, relatives, teachers, friends, or even physicians, could control this, only she could. Finally she was so thin and eating so little that her parents became concerned and began to pay a lot of attention to her weight loss. Now she realized that things between her and her parents had changed. She had become something more than an inconspicuous fifteen-year-old girl who wanted to be attractively thin.

She discovered something that comparatively few fifteen-year-old girls discover. Just by not eating she now has control, or power, over some very important people in her life, especially her parents. As she continues to lose weight, this control extends to other relatives, teachers, some of her friends, and to the doctor and others she has been sent to for help. She's pleased that even strangers begin to notice what she believes is her beauty, although it is actually her emaciation.

Now the tiger of anorexia whom she let move into her house is no longer that fun tiger he once was. But he's still a powerful tiger and he keeps telling her that even if it isn't much fun anymore not to kick him out. As long as he is with her, she'll still rule the roost even if it isn't nearly as much fun as it used to be. For Starr and many young women like her, drunk on the power they feel as the whole world seems to dance around them begging them to eat, she hangs on to the tiger.

To keep this power, and the pleasure she gets from it, the more everyone, especially her parents, begs her to eat, the more she pays attention to the tiger who keeps telling her, *Listen to me, keep pushing your food away and watch them all keep dancing to our tune.* The satisfaction associated with this newly found power negates the pain of starvation. She doesn't even feel hungry; if you ask her, she'll tell you she feels full.

Why starving is addicting to Starr and not to others is no more known than why one identical twin becomes an alcoholic and the other does not. The tendency may be in her genes, as the tendency to drink is in some alcoholics' genes. But just because the tendency is in their genes, that doesn't mean everyone with that tendency will become an addict.

The good news is that more anorexics than alcoholics or gamblers recover; in fact, most do. Some may return to normal eating; many have to be careful for years to be mindful that food is necessary. But who can and who can't go back to normal eating is not the focus of this discussion. The focus is what her parents can do with this information to persuade Starr to stop choosing to starve herself.

In order to succeed at this, they first have to do the same thing that I have suggested to other parents in this book: make a concerted effort to get closer to Starr. I need to help them to learn how to love her and still avoid getting entangled in Starr's anorexic web by trying to make her eat. Any effort to control her triggers her resistance to control that satisfies her addictive need for power. As do all the teens in this book, Starr needs parental love, not control.

But because Starr is involved in a life-threatening addiction, she does need some control. Just as an alcoholic needs a program to separate from alcohol, Starr needs a program that will reunite her with food in all the ways that the clinic she attends has figured out. If she absolutely refuses to eat, the clinic, not her parents, will force-feed her in a hospital to keep her alive. If Starr asks her parents why she is being force-fed, they should tell her that they have no choice but to support what the clinicians suggest is needed and say, "We love you. We don't want you to die."

In the last chapter, I advised Joan to visit Jackie and be loving no matter how Jackie complained but not to remove her from custody. I would advise Ed and Sara to do the same with Starr. Support the treatment program no matter how much she complains, but make no personal effort to make her eat. Whatever control she needs can be directed by caring clinicians from the treatment program. What Starr needs from her parents is their love; what she doesn't need from them is their control.

THE MEETING WITH ED AND SARA

Before I met with Ed and Sara, I had to figure out how to approach them. They would have read the first two chapters and what I've written so far in this chapter. But I was afraid they were going to take exception to my statement that what Starr needed was love, not control, because the control part of that statement wouldn't register. They would think I was intimating that they didn't love her enough. I had to be prepared for them to tell me that no parents could be more loving, that they'd devoted their lives to her anorexia for the past year, and so on. Somehow, I would have to make the point that there is a difference between just loving her and loving her to make her eat. This is a difference that is hard for parents of anorexics to understand.

Ed and Sara came in and Sara was holding in her hand the material I'd given them to read. They were a nice-looking couple in their early forties, but it was obvious the ordeal with Sara was taking its toll. They looked worried and, as I feared by the way Sara was clutching the material I'd sent them, seemed a little bothered by what they had read.

They started by telling me the story of Starr and her anorexia. It was a typical story; there was nothing remarkable about it. They told me that they'd done a lot of thinking about when it had begun and could now see that that had been almost two years ago. But they hadn't really noticed it until a little over a year ago when it became apparent she was hardly eating. As they told me this, I noted to myself that that was when it had changed from dieting to the addiction of anorexia. They had taken her to their pediatrician, who put her through all the tests and then told them the diagnosis. He referred her to the clinic and she'd been under their care for almost a year. The best they could say was that Starr was maintaining her weight but she was painfully thin.

I started by asking what they thought about what they'd read.

Ed said, "It's all very interesting, like she's addicted to that behavior, whatever that means. But all you said for us to do was love her and not get involved in her eating."

Sara broke in, "She's starving herself in front of our eyes and you tell us not to get involved in her eating. How do you expect us to do that? But it's the *you should love her more* suggestion that bothers both of us. I don't know how we could love her any more than we do."

There it was, as I had feared. They didn't see the difference between love and control. It's very hard for most loving parents to make this distinction. I said, "I was worried when I wrote that. I knew you've been very loving parents and you'd have difficulty understanding what I meant. That's why it's so important that we talk today. It's what you just said, 'I don't know how we could love her any more than we do.' I'm not asking you to love her any more. I don't doubt your love for her for a minute. Maybe what Othello said in describing his love for Desdemona, as 'one that loved not wisely but too well,' expresses what I am trying to tell you. Please, we should talk about this."

They both looked at me. I knew they were well educated, and that there was a good chance they were familiar with that famous quote, but I asked to make sure, "You've heard of that quote?" They nodded that they had and still waited for more explanation. "Remember, right at the end of that material I gave you, I said she needs your love, she doesn't need your control. I believe what Shakespeare was trying to explain through Othello's speech was that wise love is not controlling love. Please, I'm not doubting your love but tell me, even if you don't say it to Starr, what message do you, both of you, send strongly to her when you sit down to a meal?"

There was a long pause, then Sara said, "I can't look at her and not want to get her to eat."

Ed added, "We're afraid if we weren't after her all the time, she wouldn't eat anything."

"Do either of you really think she eats more because you're after her?"

They looked at each other. They were beginning to get what I was trying to explain. Sara said, "That stuff about external control and the deadly habits. We don't really criticize or blame but I guess we complain about her not eating and we nag a lot."

Ed followed with, "But how can we help it? I mean there she is starving herself."

"Do you talk to her about food? Do you make special food for her?"

Sara said, "We try not to. But our whole house revolves around food and how much she eats."

"Right now who's in control of your whole house, you or her?"

Ed admitted, "She is."

"Who knows more about food, calories, portion size, fat content, vitamins, you or Starr?"

Sara explained, "But even if we don't say anything, she brings it up. She has a dozen books on nutrition."

Ed said, "Are you suggesting we shouldn't talk to her when she wants to talk about food?"

"It's hard to suggest exactly what you should do. I know the pressure you're under all the time. But my feeling is that food, even her not eating, isn't the real problem. She knows more about food and how to eat it or not eat it than you'll know if you live another hundred years. Talking to her about food is like talking to Michael Jordan about basketball."

Ed said quickly, "But what'll we do if we stop focusing on food?"

"It may sound a little stilted but I think she has to hear it from you. Tell her you love her but you're going to stop talking to her about food and you're going to stop preparing meals with her in mind. But also tell her it's not important to you that she eats what you're eating. As far as you're concerned she can eat anything she wants. Or any amount of anything she wants. She can go with you to the store and you'll buy it or go by herself if she wants to. If she wants to, she can cook her own food. But from now on you're not going to talk about food. Her food and her eating is up to her."

Sara said, "Wouldn't that seem strange after all we've been doing?"

I said, "I'm hoping it'll seem strange to her, strange enough so she'll pay attention. But no more strange than talking about food all day long to someone who doesn't want to eat. Just phase food out of your conversations. Leave all the food talk up to the clinic she's going to. Do you talk about anything else that has to do with her problem, like how she's doing in school?"

Ed said, "Well, she misses a lot of school; we don't talk much to her about it but she can see we're worried about it."

"Okay, stop worrying about school. School's not the problem either. When she starts to eat, she'll catch up. How about her health? Do you talk much about that?"

Sara said, "We ask her how she feels. We do that all the time."

"Can't you tell how she feels? Doesn't she say 'fine,' when you know she isn't feeling fine?"

Sara said, "You're trying to tell us we ought to stay out of her anorexia. Like pretend it doesn't exist?"

"Look, I'm not telling you anything you don't know by now. Her anorexia will exist as long as she wants it to, and there isn't a thing you can do about it. She could start eating today if she wanted to. My opinion is the more you're concerned about it, the less she'll eat. After all this time, do you think that one of these days you'll be able to talk her into eating?"

Ed said, "You're not talking about some kid in the neighborhood. She's our child. You want us to ignore her problem."

"That's exactly what I want you to do. What I'd like to see you do is pay attention to her as if she didn't have this problem. I was trying to explain it in what you read. Do you see the difference?"

Sara said, "I see it when you say it. But when I look at her emaciated body I can't seem to see it at all."

"Do you remember what I said in the first chapter was the only human problem?"

Sara said, "Yes, you said it was unhappiness. That seemed way too simplistic to us."

Ed nodded in agreement.

"It is simple. I like things simple. Things that are simple are easy to understand. The clinic's treating Starr for anorexia. That's real complicated. I'll bet you don't understand much about what they're doing, do you?"

Sara said, "Not really; they've given us some books to read, but most of what the books explain is stuff we already know from just watching Starr."

"Simple as it may sound, do you think Starr's unhappy?"

Ed said, "Of course she's unhappy. She's starving herself. How could she be happy?"

"That's a real good question. How could a person who's starving herself be happy? I'd like to focus on that question for a few minutes. Do you remember what I said is the cause of human unhappiness?"

Sara said, "I remember it exactly. You said people are unhappy when they can't get along with the important people in their lives the way they want to."

Ed said, "You explained that they try to force the people they can't get along with to do things they don't want to do. That's the external control Sara mentioned a few minutes ago."

"Do you think that Starr is exempt from that problem? Who are the important people in her life?"

Ed said, "We are. She's an only child. She really doesn't have anyone else." Sara nodded.

I said, "Every day for the past year, whenever you're together with Starr, does she seem to enjoy it when you ask her how she feels or if she's hungry or if she wants more to eat?"

Sara said, "She makes a face."

Ed said, "Most of the time she doesn't even answer."

"But you keep bringing it up."

Sara said, "But if she doesn't want us to talk about it, she'd start to eat."

"Exactly. So maybe for all the faces she makes and her pretending not to hear what you say to her, she wants you to talk about her and her problem. Like you said, the whole family revolves around her eating. As long as she doesn't eat, she's able to control every thought you have about her and every word that comes out of your mouths. Don't you ever get the feeling that she's getting something out of not eating?"

Sara said, "I do, I've felt that for a long time."

Ed said, "We both do. We've talked about that. But what we can't figure out is why she'd want to control us. She was always so easy to get along with before all this started."

"Don't you want to control her? Isn't all your talk about her eating to control her?"

Ed said, "But it's different. We're her parents. We're trying to control her because we love her."

"I'm sure you love her. We've already talked about that. But when did she really cut down on her eating? You already told me; do you remember when?"

Sara said, "When we took her to the doctor. When we got the diagnosis."

Ed said, "When we sent her to the clinic."

"Do you remember what I said in the first chapter? What do most people do when you try to control them?"

Sara thought for a moment and said, "They resist, I remember that." Ed nodded.

"Now here's the point of the first chapter. When people resist, what happens to the relationship between them and the people who are trying to control them?"

They both said, "It harms it."

"It's like a contest. Teenagers do it with their parents all the time. But in this contest Starr is doing more than resisting. She's upped the ante. She's decided she wants to control you and she's succeeding. She's winning the contest and winning feels good. When she tells you she's not hungry, she's telling you the truth. It feels so good to be in charge of the whole house that she's become addicted to that feeling. I wrote about that; now I'm trying to explain it. Besides, she can't lose because she knows you love her so much. The cards are stacked against you. The more you try to control her, the less she eats. The less she eats, the more you control. Do you want to keep doing this forever?"

Sara said, "But she may die; anorexia can be fatal. We can't give up."

"Do you think the clinic you're sending her to is going to let her die? Have they told you she's very close to death right now?"

Ed said, "No, they tell us she's a little better."

"So why don't you let them handle her anorexia and you go back to being her parents and start worrying about your relationship with her. Break the cycle you're in with her. Enjoy her, love her, do things with her, tell her to invite her friends over, and don't say a word about her eating problem if any of them come. I think she needs both of you very much but not so much she'll stop fighting your constant effort to control her."

Sara said, "But she started it. We didn't start it. I hate to keep repeating myself but if she didn't want us to control her, why'd she stop eating? If she'd eat, we'd stop."

"What you say makes perfect sense to me and to you. But unfortunately it doesn't make sense to Starr: You didn't start it, she did. But what difference does it really make who started it? What makes sense now is for you to stop it. I think she started out to be thin but very quickly it shifted to a battle for control. Why she made this shift from trying to lose some weight to a power struggle with you I don't think anyone knows. What I do know is it takes two to contest something. If you're willing to give up, the contest can come to an end."

Ed still wasn't satisfied; he said, "But this is crazy. There must be a reason."

"Ed, you're dealing with human nature and the need for power. We fought a whole war in Vietnam that started for one reason but quickly escalated into a power struggle to prove no little Asian country could control us, and now we're friends with them. If you ask Starr her reason for starving herself, she'll tell you it was to be more attractive. She will no more realize she's now in a war for control than the initiators of the Vietnam War realized it until long after the war was over. In marriage a war may start over the toilet seat being left up and escalate into divorce."

Sara said, "Can you guarantee we won't lose her if we stop urging her to eat?"

"No, I can't guarantee anything. If you didn't have good clinicians watching her anorexia very closely, I'd be hesitant to suggest what I've just suggested. But right now you don't need to deal with her eating problem, you can stop. She may even want to start eating again but won't as long as you keep doing what you've been doing. If she starts eating or makes any move in that direction, don't say a thing. If she asks you why you aren't saying anything, tell her you love her whether she eats or not. Do you think you can do it?"

Ed said, "What do you think, Sara?"

"It'll be hard but I think it's worth a try. They did tell us at the clinic to let them handle it. They've told her that if her weight goes below ninety pounds she'll have to be force-fed. I hated the idea but I guess they're right. She is holding just above ninety."

"Try it for a few weeks and then come back and let's talk some more, okay?"

As they were leaving, Ed said, "I think it'd be a good idea if we read that material over again."

NINE

TEENAGE DRUG ADDICTION—SACRIFICING HAPPINESS FOR PLEASURE

In this chapter, I would like to use the problem of drug addiction to explain the difference between happiness and pleasure. Parents who understand that difference have the best chance of helping a teen who uses or is even addicted to a drug. When an addicting drug enters the brain of a person who is looking for pleasure, the drug by itself can provide more intense, reliable pleasure than any other human experience.

The only human experience that comes close to providing this much pleasure is the sexual pleasure that can occur between two strongly attracted, sexually motivated partners. But because the intensity of sexual pleasure depends a lot on the freshness of the attraction and on the mutual sexual motivation, this pleasure is rarely as reliable or as intense day after day for years on end as an addicting drug is to an addict.

What an addicting drug cannot provide is the happiness of the far less intense but longer-lasting pleasure of a satisfying relationship, with or without sexual involvement. While all relationships have ups and downs, a satisfying marriage or satisfying parent-child relationship can provide pleasure and happiness for a lifetime.

But for either of these relationships to be happy, the power in the relationship must be reasonably close to balanced. What I've shown so far in this book is that parents who want to get along with their teens need to relinquish a lot of the power that most parents believe they need to have if this relationship is to succeed. The paradox is that the more direct control a parent is willing to give up, the more indirect control he or she gains through the stronger and happier relationship.

For example, Starr, in the last chapter, who had gained a great deal of power over her parents when she stopped eating, also benefited from her parents' taking the first step by reducing their efforts to make her eat. For her to give up her anorexia, she had to relinquish some power. But she would not do so until they had given up some of theirs while continuing to love her. If you as a parent are willing to do this, your teen will tend to see it as you giving him or her more love and a chance for the happiness the teen needs to stay away from the pleasure of addiction.

This is a lesson I've been trying to teach to almost every parent appearing in the book. But as we have seen with Ed and Sara, it is a very difficult lesson for parents to learn because it goes against all they've believed about child rearing since their child was born. If your teen is involved with an addicting drug, learning this lesson may be the only way you can persuade your child to give up drugs. In any unsatisfying teen-parent relationship, your teen's appreciation of your parental love is the strongest thing you have going for you. It isn't a case of your giving up all your power; it's more a case of your being willing to balance it between the two of you.

The nature of drug addiction is that once a person is addicted to a lifestyle-destroying drug, such as alcohol, cocaine, methedrine, or heroin, that person will willingly sacrifice his or her happiness for the more predictable, one could even say more sure, pleasure of the drug. I say more sure because what makes a drug addicting is its ability to go right to the pleasure centers of the brain with no need for a less certain starting place outside the brain.

For example, the use of the drug makes it unnecessary for the addict to try for the good feelings associated with the love, power, and freedom inherent in the effort of achieving a good relationship. Under the influence of alcohol, heroin, cocaine, or methedrine, the addict, be he a parent or a teenager, may be willing to sacrifice the parent-child relationship for the pleasure of the drug. An addiction to these drugs can do something no other human experience can do: destroy the relationship between a parent and a child.

Unlike happiness, which must be nurtured if it is to be strong, all the drug addict has to do to get pleasure is use the drug and, for more pleasure, use more of it. It is the search for pleasure beyond what the drug can provide that leads an addict to an overdose and death.

In an addict's quality world, the only important picture is that of the pleasure to be gained from the drug. All other pictures are subordinate to that picture. If there is a cure for drug addiction, and I believe in many cases there is, it comes as a result of persuading the addict to include at least one person in his quality world, in a more important place than his picture of the drug experience. In the case of a teen using drugs, the picture that has the best chance of taking precedence over the drug is the picture of him and at least one of his parents relating enjoyably to each other.

If you are the parent of a teen, even a preteen, you should accept as fact that your child will be offered a drug, usually alcohol at first, by someone who will tell him that he should not miss this great experience. That messenger will usually tell your teen that he himself is not addicted. He can stop anytime he wants to. He will tell your child not to worry, the drug is safe if used the way he does. He will also tell your teen that if he wants to get pleasure from heroin, he has to be patient and give the drug a chance. There may be some discomfort at first but, if he keeps trying, he will soon feel the pleasure and that early pain will not appear again. Any teen who stays with this drug past the initial discomfort has a good chance of becoming addicted.

There is no sure way to predict in advance who will get hooked. But the better the teen gets along with one or both parents, the less likely he is to get hooked. Getting along well with your teen means that he feels free to talk with you about all the choices he is making with his life, including the choice to try a drug and to get involved with sex. John's loving talk with his father, Ken, in chapter 4, about his sexual relationship with Alexis, was a strong deterrent to his overuse of any drug.

If your teen can talk freely with you and believe you are not judging him or trying to control him, he will be more likely to listen to your advice and there is less chance that he will become addicted. The choice theory—involving no external control and total-communication parenting—I've been explaining in this book has a better chance of helping him avoid addiction to drugs than anything else I know.

You as a parent may be in one or more of three situations that could make it difficult for you to talk with your teen about drugs: (1) you may be a total abstainer, (2) you may be a user, or (3) you may be addicted yourself. If you are lucky enough to be a nonuser, except for caffeine and nicotine, your nonuse will speak for itself. It will speak louder than anything you can say as long as you are careful not to point out how virtuous you are.

At all costs, avoid saying, "Since I don't do it, I won't stand for you doing it either." By now you should be well aware that all the deadly habits stop communication with your teen and that criticism is the deadliest of those habits. If he wants to talk to you about drugs, listen more than you talk if you can possibly do it. Keep in mind that in this area, external control is so much in the air between you that even if you don't use it, he may still hear anything you say as controlling.

Nicotine is, perhaps, the most addicting drug there is. It may kill the teen, but that death is far down the road. Don't jeopardize your relationship with him by making a big external control deal out of smoking except to say that the rule is there's no smoking in your house. Of course that goes for you as well as him. If you have a good relationship with him, there's a good chance he'll stop smoking while his health is still good. If you don't have a good relationship, he may go on to other drugs or other self-destructive activities that may be as much the result of a bad relationship as the fact he is smoking.

In this day and age, if you smoke, most likely you're addicted. Talk to the teen honestly about your addiction and, if it's the truth, tell him you'd like to quit and ask him to help you by keeping close with you. Explain some choice theory to him so he knows how important he is to you. Nothing you can do will make more of an impression on him than how good he'll feel if he helps you to quit. Your improved relationship will help both of you and may help him to be wary of all addicting drugs in the future. If you go to a stop-smoking program, ask him to come with you. Seeing him there trying to help you, will help everyone. The idea of a teen helping his parent or parents is a too long neglected part of the teen-parent relationship.

If you use alcohol socially, as many parents do, be honest with the your teen while she is in grade school about the use and misuse of alcohol. This may not prevent the teen from overdoing it but it will pave the way for honest discussions when the teen starts to drink. If you expect your teen to be abstinent until she is twenty-one, all you will do is destroy the communication with you that she will need long before she reaches the legal age for drugs and sex.

We live in a real world. The joys of sex and alcohol are portrayed on television directly and indirectly every day. The only protection you can offer your child is your relationship with her, and never underestimate that relationship. Without her parents anchored strongly in her quality world, your teen goes unarmed into a life filled with hazards.

If you use marijuana, your teen will know about it. Even if you are not addicted to it—and it is likely you are not, as compared even with caffeine this is not a highly addicting drug—you will have to talk to her about your use of it. She will be exposed to it in her milieu almost as much as to alcohol. Talk to your teen about the problems of using: the cost, the danger (because it is illegal), and the small but still real danger of addiction. Again, no preaching.

This talk will be so uncomfortable for many parents who smoke pot that it has a better chance of persuading the parent or parents to stop than anything else they may do. If you decide to stop, wait for a while to make sure you've actually quit before telling your teen. She doesn't need to see you fail.

If you are a parent who uses cocaine or heroin recreationally but are not addicted and your teen doesn't know about your habit, I wouldn't bring this up. The life of a teenager is hard enough without having to deal with your problem. But if they do know about it, I'd be honest and tell them all you give up for this habit, especially the money. But whether you are a user or an addict, no matter how much you may protest that you love your daughter, the drug to you is more important than your child, and likely more important than your mate or anyone else.

Your teen will soon figure out that she is less important to you than the drug. Your use is doing great harm to your relationship; you are the worst kind of a role model. My advice is to get into treatment or be willing to kiss your child, and very likely your marriage, good-bye.

Obviously, if you are the parent of a teen, you are a role model. The closer you are to what you'd like your teen to be, in most instances, the better. But if you model a life that your teen has difficulty relating to as Ken did with John in chapter 4, don't depend on your teen to help you out as John did Ken. I also wouldn't count on your teen turning out the way you want if you put too much pressure on him to be like you.

Where drugs are concerned, what I'm pointing out is a rather narrow road, with not much room for flexibility, but share what you are doing with your teen and try to reduce your dependence on any drug you may use. If you are stuck, ask her for suggestions. It is a good way to empower her and if she comes up with a good suggestion for you, make a real effort to follow it. If you aren't willing to follow what she suggests, don't ask for suggestions.

Remember, as I've tried to point out in this chapter, your children need you but you need them, too. Don't take a chance on harming your relationship by replacing honesty with external control.

TEN

DEALING WITH A TEEN WHO'S BEEN LABELED SCHIZOPHRENIC

In the psychiatric world, there is some disagreement over what schizophrenia actually is. The largest group of psychiatrists consider all disorders to be organically based. They believe that all mental illnesses—for example, schizophrenia, depression, bipolar disorder, and obsessive-compulsive disorder—are caused by something physically or chemically wrong with the brain. They believe that these illnesses can be best treated by psychiatric drugs, which change the neurochemistry of the brain, and they tend to prescribe these brain drugs based as much on what family members tell them about the patient's condition as on extensive conversation with the patients themselves.

By now I'm sure you've gathered that I am a member of the opposite group. As I explained in chapter 2, most of us believe that the symptoms labeled in current literature as mental illness are not caused by damage to the brain and its chemistry. They are descriptions of the many ways that teens or adults who are diagnosed as mentally ill choose to deal with what I believe is the basic human problem: unhappiness. This group of psychiatrists is led by Peter Breggin, M.D., and the book he wrote in 1991 is still as valid as the day he wrote it.*

We believe, as I explain in *Choice Theory,* that you can have a normal brain and still choose to be extremely unhappy and choose some extreme symptoms such as the craziness of schizophrenia. But as I explained in the first two chapters of the book you are now reading, the basic cause of your unhappiness is an unsatisfying relationship often coupled with a failure to succeed at what you want to do with your life.

For example, as explained in the previous chapter, drug addiction is not a mental illness caused by brain malfunctioning. It is a search for pleasure or relief from pain, engaged in by first disconnected, then addicted, people. The cure is to do much more than to take away their addicting drug or give them drugs that stop the craving. The cure is to help them reconnect with the important people in their lives.

From your standpoint as a parent, which side of this argument you are on makes a great deal of difference as you try to figure out how to help a child who has been labeled schizophrenic. One course of action is to turn the care of your teen over to an organic psychiatrist, who will treat him with brain drugs and who may advise you that your child may never be normal again, that it is likely he will need both the drugs and some care in an institution or hospital on and off for the rest of his life. One of the few things the organic psychiatrists will tell you that I agree with, is that you are not responsible for his condition.

But as I will explain in this chapter, the psychiatric symptoms of your teen are his own particular way of dealing with his unhappiness. While he is almost always aware he is unhappy, he is rarely aware that his unhappiness is related to his inability to connect with you and other important people in his life. In fact,

---

*Peter Breggin, *Toxic Psychiatry* (New York: St. Martin's Press, 1991).

his symptoms may be his way of replacing the effort he needs to make if he is to connect with the people like you who are important are to him. His symptoms may also be related to an unrealistic fear that you are about to abandon him or send him someplace away from his home with you.

Very likely he is also totally unaware that he is choosing the crazy symptoms that are now making it almost impossible for him to reconnect with you or anyone else. He does not realize that you, his parent(s), or relatives, are his best chance for a satisfying connection. You are the person or people most concerned about him and most able to help him directly or to find help for him from a person who is skilled in helping him to reconnect. Since there is a good chance that you are the most important person in his life, what I will now explain may be of great help to you.

What will make helping your schizophrenic teen more difficult than helping any of the other teens I have described so far, is that he will be hard for you to talk with. His mind is on other things; for example, he may hear voices that are created in his own brain but which he believes are real, and he will tend to confuse what you are saying with those auditory hallucinations.

Let me now begin to explain some things about your teen that I believe are important for you to understand. For a more in-depth explanation than I have space for in this book, I suggest you read chapter 7 of my book *Choice Theory,* and chapter 10 of my subsequent book, *Counseling with Choice Theory: The New Reality Therapy.** You would do well to read both those books in their entirety.

In the first chapter of this book, I explained that we are all

---

*William Glasser, *Counseling with Choice Theory: The New Reality Therapy* (New York: HarperCollins, 2001). Published in hardcover by Harper-Collins in 2000 under the title *Reality Therapy in Action.*

driven by five genetic needs: survival, love and belonging, power, freedom, and fun. Two chapters ago, using Starr for an example, I introduced the concept of the quality world. In this chapter, I will explain the two remaining components of choice theory: *total behavior* and *creativity*. When you understand these, it should help you deal with your psychotic teen more effectively than you are now doing.

TOTAL BEHAVIOR

Choice theory explains that our behavior is made up of four individual but inseparable components: acting, thinking, feeling, and the physiology that goes along with any or all of the other three components. As I sit here, my total behavior—typing—could best be described as the following four behavioral components: I am *thinking* about what to type; *acting*, by moving my hands and my fingers; *feeling* good because I am making progress; and my heart beating, my breathing, and my brain activity make up the fourth component, my *physiology*.

Of these four components, two are under my direct control (my thinking and my acting), two are not under my direct control (my feelings and my physiology). I can indirectly control how I feel and, to lesser extent, my physiology by how I choose to think and act. While there is a very complete explanation of total behavior in the book *Choice Theory,* here all you have to know is that when you are very disconnected your creativity can get very involved in any one of the four components. When you are unhappy your creativity can get involved in your thinking and in your brain physiology. It can lead to what is commonly called psychosis or schizophrenia.

To get your creativity less involved it is necessary that you succeed in reconnecting with the people you used to be connected to or find a new person to help you as I attempted to help Teri in chapter 6. To further understand psychosis, let me now explain creativity.

CREATIVITY

Suppose your teen hands you a bad report card and then goes into a long, rambling, semicoherent story about a huge conspiracy in the school to force him to get involved in homosexual relationships with a group of teachers and because he refused they gave him the low grades. As he talks to you, he keeps looking away and then asks you, "Don't you hear them? They are talking about me right now and telling me if I don't submit to what they want, they'll expel me from school." I could write a lot more but I'm sure you could see that if that were your son, you'd be alarmed.

What's going on in your seventeen-year-old son's mind is being offered to him by his own creativity. We are all creative but this is totally frightening. All of us are aware of creativity. It is in play when any one of us is trying to figure out what to do, but few of us have an appreciation for its role in psychiatric problems. Many mental health practitioners who blame a defective brain or imbalanced brain chemistry for aberrant behavior would be more helpful if they would explain to family members, and if possible to the psychotic person himself, that his seemingly bizarre thoughts, actions, or feelings are thrust upon him by his own creativity.

In such cases, I believe that the person's creativity is desperately trying to help him find a way to deal with a situation that he is very frightened of and does not know how to deal with. But whatever that situation is, it has something to do with a present disconnection in his life or his fear of an imminent disconnection because he is not successful at his stated goal in life. As you think about this occurrence, you begin to realize that he has not been as involved recently with the family or with you, his parent or parents, as he once had been; maybe he had talked to you a little bit about his fear of going away in the fall to college.

The common delusions of persecution or hallucinations of voices accusing the psychotic person of sexually deviant behaviors are crude ways his own creativity is devising to blame his present disconnection or fear of disconnection on others and, in doing so, to reassure him it's not his fault. In extreme cases, his creativity may even think of ways he can avenge himself by killing or harming people who he believes are out to get him.

By the time that creativity takes over a person's life as it does when someone becomes psychotic or schizophrenic, that person is so unhappy that he doesn't even consider that what he's talking about is delusional or what he is hearing is hallucinatory. In working with psychotic people, if we would stop thinking in terms of mental illness caused by brain damage and think, instead, in terms of bizarre creativity, we would understand much more about what's really going on.

I think we could reach many more of these disconnected people than we are reaching now if we'd talk to them more and place less emphasis on drugs to cure an illness of the brain many of us don't believe exists. If your teen has been diagnosed as schizophrenic and is on medication, the purpose of these drugs is to reduce the creativity and make his thinking less bizarre. I don't suggest you take your child off the drugs or do anything other than what your doctor recommends. I do strongly suggest that you make a real effort to talk with your psychotic teen— but try not to get involved in his bizarre creativity. This may seem to be more difficult than it really is. Let me explain what I mean.

CRAIG AND MAUREEN

Seventeen-year-old Craig, a senior, had been a very good student in an excellent California high school. He'd had high scores on his SATs and was admitted to a major university for the fall. During the summer, soon after he graduated from high school and was waiting for college to start in the fall, he became secretive and isolated from his mother, with whom he lived. An older brother was out on his own and doing well but had little interest in Craig. Whenever he came home, which was not very often, he called him a nerd. All through the school year, Craig worked in a local bookstore and was planning to work there all summer.

But soon after school ended, he quit his job and told his mother that the manager of the bookstore was trying to read his mind. When his mother asked why he now stayed in his room all the time, he said he was working on a project that would change the world. He stopped bathing and shaving, started staying up all night, and slept in his clothes during the day. He'd had a few good friends in high school, but they soon stopped coming to see him and began telling Maureen that Craig needed help.

She took him to a psychiatrist, who put him on drugs, told her he was schizophrenic, and said he might have to be put into a group home if he started to go out and bother people in the community. He also offered to refer him for care in a day-care center for mental patients, but Craig wouldn't go and there was no way she could make him go.

Maureen noticed that as long as she didn't try to push him

to do anything, including bathe and shave, he wasn't hostile. But if she tried to persuade him to do anything for himself, he told her with some hostility to leave him alone and that, if she kept bothering him, he'd move to New York, a place he'd never been. He seemed a little less agitated on the medication but there was no significant improvement.

When she came to see me for advice, she told me all of the above and asked, "But what do I do? He just sits in his room. I can't always get him to come out for dinner. His doctor says I should be patient and keep him on the medication. I feel so helpless. I keep reading in the paper about all these miraculous new drugs for mental illness. Where are they?"

"There is nothing miraculous in the drug area but there are some things you can do that may help over and above doing what the doctor told you. Basically, what Craig's done is cut himself off from the people he needs. Psychosis, which I prefer to call it, or schizophrenia, as it is mostly called, is a condition of loneliness in which the sufferer isolates himself from the rest of the world. As he separates himself from people, he gets more and more creatively involved with his own brain. He's using this self-involvement to replace the people he very much needs."

"I don't understand what you're talking about. How can you get involved with your own brain?"

I then explained what appears earlier in this chapter, how people who are psychotic get involved with their own creativity, and then repeated myself in the hopes she would now understand what I was trying to explain. "As I just said, he's using this involvement to replace the people he needs. Very creative people such as Einstein and Mozart did this all the time. The difference is they knew they were disconnecting temporarily and he doesn't. He probably hears voices and thinks they are real people. Maybe the medication has turned off the voices, but he has no people in his life to replace them with. In a sense the medication has made him less disordered but may have left him more lonely. Like I explained, right now he's disconnected."

"But how did he get disconnected? He didn't have a lot of friends in high school but he did have a few very good friends. You know, he hung around with good students like himself but there're not that many of those."

"Did he have a girlfriend?"

"He had girlfriends but never a girlfriend in that sense of the word."

"Did he have any fear of leaving here and going off to college?"

"He didn't seem to. All he talked about during the school year was going to college."

"Was that recently? I mean at the end of the school year or was it more last fall?"

"It might have been more last fall. He doesn't talk about it now at all."

"Do you think he might be scared? I mean scared to go off by himself to college. I don't like to call him schizophrenic, it seems so permanent. I like to think he had a nervous breakdown and maybe he can be helped. Breakdowns are not unusual for very good students like Craig. Some of them are scared stiff of entering the unfamiliar world of college. A hundred years ago it was so common at the end of adolescence that it used to be called dementia praecox or early dementia. Do you bring up the subject of college at all to him?"

"I used to. But then I noticed he got real agitated so I've mostly stopped. It's funny because last fall he wanted to talk about it all the time."

"Does he ever mention anything about his friends who are going off to college soon?"

"He hasn't but once in a while, but I think I might have brought it up."

"There's been a lot of research to indicate that it's more the social unknown of college than the academic unknown, but it's probably both that he fears. Did he ever give you the impression that he'd changed his mind about college?"

"He stopped talking about it but he still hasn't come right out and said he doesn't want to go."

"How do you feel about him not going to college this fall?"

"You really think he won't go to college this year?"

"What does it look like to you?"

"But he wanted it so much."

"With all he talked about it, it's hard for him to face and he may be too frightened to go. Somewhere in his mind he may still think he's going to go. But I wonder if he really doesn't think he's not ready to go. Do you think this breakdown may be a way for him to tell you?"

"But, it's crazy. I have no intention of trying to make him go to college."

"It may not be as crazy as you think. When did you last bring up the subject of college?"

"Are you intimating that it's my fault, that I've been pushing him to go to college?"

"No, not pushing him. There's nothing abnormal about the mother of a good student like Craig wanting him to go to a good college. And being thrilled when he got in. I'll bet all the parents of good students in his high school push their kids toward college."

"But what'll he do if he doesn't go to college?"

"He's doing something now."

"You call schizophrenia doing something?"

"I think all behavior including crazy behavior has a purpose. Remember, what he's doing and thinking is not crazy to Craig. It's not even crazy to me; I've dealt with a lot of it. I can't blame you for thinking it's crazy but it's not what you think or I think, it's what he thinks, that counts."

"But what do I do?"

"You could try to get over the feeling you have to do something."

"What do you mean by that?"

"I mean there isn't anything you can really do except love him and talk to him. You can't make him stop being creative. Isn't the idea that he's being creative so much better than the idea he's crazy?"

"I don't know."

"Tell me: When you made this appointment to see me, what was really on your mind?"

"You think I had something on my mind besides helping Craig?"

"I think it'd be normal to have something very much on your mind when you came to see me. Could you tell me what it was?"

"If you're so smart, you tell me."

"My guess is you were hoping that I could help you get Craig to be able to get started in college this coming fall. But by now, I'd guess you'd settle for the second semester."

"You want me to get that thought out of my head?"

"I'd like you to do more than that. If you really don't care if he doesn't go to college this year, I'd like you to tell Craig. Tell him you'll wait until he's ready."

"But won't he think I'm rejecting him, if I give up on his going to college this fall?"

"I don't think he'll feel you're rejecting him if you tell him what he wants to hear. Believe me, this is not an unusual situation. There's a better chance he'll feel you accept him more if you tell him you won't be disappointed. It could help him a lot if you mean it. You don't have to get college out of your mind forever. But if you could forget about it for this year, it might help a lot. Has he ever mentioned anything he'd like to do this year besides go to college?"

"He loved working in that bookstore. I was heartbroken when he quit."

"You might bring up the bookstore in a conversation but not about him going back. Just bring it up by saying something like doesn't he miss the bookstore. It would be like you're accepting that as something he might do if he doesn't go to college. Which of course I hope is okay with you. What he needs is to talk with you without feeling he has to do something to please you. Forget about what you want for a while and try to find out what he wants. Some kids need direction. Right now, I think he needs nondirection. And if you can get him out of the house even for a walk, it would be good for him. If he goes, don't feel you have to do anything but walk with him. And don't say anything like, 'Don't you feel better to be out walking?' Keep that idea of nondirection in mind."

I've counseled some kids like Craig, temporarily psychotic but they get over it, and I've been pretty successful. "Going crazy" is not uncommon for young people when they feel disconnected or fear they will soon be, as Craig may feel. Ophelia became psychotic when she couldn't connect with Hamlet. But she was brutally rejected. Maureen won't do anything like that with Craig.

The next thing she might do, if she can, is find a young man who's going to the local junior college and hire him to spend some nondirectional but mutually enjoyable time with Craig. It would be good for Craig to see that the university is not the be-all and the end-all; there are other places that offer a good start toward an education. A possibility for Craig would be to spend two years in a junior college near home, allowing him to get over his fear, and then transfer to the university. What Craig needs right now is a connection with someone new, with whom he doesn't have to feel inferior just because he wants to postpone college.

I have no more suggestions for Maureen. Keep in mind that when we are disconnected or fear we will soon be disconnected, we are capable of some very destructive or self-destructive creativity. If you have an immature but hardworking, studious teen like Craig, don't be surprised if he is afraid of the university. And if he's pushing himself, try not to burden him with your expectations. That is exactly what he doesn't need right now.

ELEVEN

IF THEY'D TEACH US LIKE THAT, WE'D ALL LEARN

As much as I'm enjoying writing this book, I wasn't looking forward to writing this chapter. I'm sad just contemplating what I have to tell almost all of the parents who read this book. In chapter 3, where I advised Kim on how to deal with Jody, I felt on solid ground because I did not focus on the question Kim is sure to ask me when we get together again. But here she is today, and the first thing she has told me is that she and Jody are getting along better than they have in a year.

She said, "I don't worry as much as I did about the parties because we're now on very frank terms about sex and drugs. I laid my cards on the table, told her that I love her but I can't protect her. She's told me that I had every right to be concerned, she's concerned, too. She's even talked to a lot of her friends about our new closeness and how honest we are with each other, and a lot of them have come over and talked to me about how I'm treating Kim. They all stress that they don't want to ruin their lives. I feel very comfortable with that part of my problem."

But then Jody asked me the question I'd been fearing. She said, "It's not only Jody, all the girls Jody hangs around with keep telling me they hate school. They really don't want an answer, they know I don't know that much about school. But they just keep complaining and I don't know what to say."

I asked, "Don't they like anything about school? Do they hate it all?"

"I asked them about that and they said, they go for the social life and they do like some of the teachers. What they hate are the homework and the tests, what goes on in the classroom. There's a huge amount of memorizing stuff and no one tells them when they'll ever use it. But most of all they hate math, especially algebra. It's a total mystery to almost all of them, they don't even know what it is. And I can't help Jody. I'm an accountant, I know how to add, subtract, all the basic arithmetic, but algebra's as much a mystery to me as it is to Jody. I tell her to go ask her father but she still won't go into that house. But I'm working on that. Now that we're getting along so well, I don't even hate him anymore."

When she asked me that question, I became very sad, not because I can't answer it but because I can. There is an answer to Kim's question about school. I have spent more time working in schools for the last forty years than almost any other expert and I am a recognized authority on education. As of the year 2000, I know what could be done that would change school into a place where Jody, Teri, Robert, and John, all the kids in this book who hate school, would like it.

They would like it there because they would like the teachers and the way they were being taught. They'd get good grades and high scores on the state tests that all the politicians are so worried about. What I know would work in minority schools as well as or better than it would work in the middle-class school that Jody and her friends attend. Discipline problems would disappear and it would all cost less than we are spending now.

When I explained this to Kim, she said, "I don't believe you."

I answered, "That's why I'm so sad. You think that there's nothing that can be done that'll come close to what I'm saying could be done. But what I'm most sad about is that many educators all over the world are listening to me. They buy my books and they read them. They invite me to speak to their teachers and I get a lot of applause when I make my presentation. But only a few schools actually try to put what I suggest into practice. They don't even say it's hard to do. What they tell me is it's so different from what they've ever done that they're reluctant to try it. I don't even want to explain it to you because you'll say what five tenth-graders, who were doing poorly in school, said when I explained it to them in front of an audience of fifteen hundred teachers in the Midwest about a year ago. All five of them looked at me and one by one said some version of, 'But if they'd teach that way everybody would learn.' And the others agreed. A lot of the teachers agreed but nothing much has happened."

Kim said, "Is this written down?"

"It's in my latest book on education called *Every Student Can Succeed*. It describes what I call a Glasser Quality School. There are eight of them around the country with another hundred trying. If I could say to you that there's absolutely nothing that can be done to make school a better place, I wouldn't be so sad. But it could be done easily if we'd be willing to do something very different. We are stuck with a school tradition that doesn't work. We've got to break that tradition, and parents like you could help. Parents are the only force schools respond to."

But for now I have to help Kim deal with Jody's school problem. I said, "Kim, I'd like to role-play. You play Jody and I'll play you. I think you may be able to help her where she is by offering what I suggest. Can we get started?"

"Sure, go ahead."

"Jody, what's the worst thing about school?"

"Boring, boring, boring."

"Okay, I agree. It was boring for me, too. If I'd been better at school, I'd be a CPA and we'd have a lot more money. Do you think I'm smart enough to have done better in school?"

"Is this your way of asking if I'm smart?"

"Okay, I admit it. Are you?"

"Of course I am. I don't do anything and I get C's. I think I could learn algebra if the teacher would slow down and give us a chance to learn it. He just rushes along and about ten nerds are with him. I've stopped asking questions because he says he answered that question a week ago, you should have paid attention. But he won't fail me. If he failed kids like me, he'd have so many back next year he wouldn't know what to do."

"Okay, it's the boring I'm worried about. Do you know why you're so bored in school?"

"It's the same thing, over and over. Nothing's ever new."

"Would you be more interested if it wasn't always the same? Like in art, you do different things."

"It's the teachers. They lecture, give homework and tests. It's all the same. The clock goes so slow I think it's stuck. Every period is a hundred years long."

"You say the teachers are all the same. How about the kids? Are they all the same?"

"Pretty much. Sometimes one of the boys talks back or drops a book. But he gets thrown out and has Saturday detention. I keep my mouth shut. That's how I get my C's."

"So if the teacher's the same and the kids are the same, how could it not be boring?"

"You don't want me to get into trouble, do you?"

"No, but if the teachers never change and you want something different, it has to be up to you to do something different and still not get into trouble."

"Okay, what do you suggest I do?"

"What's the most boring subject?"

"General science. Basically he lectures from the book, and all the test questions are from the book. And the homework is to read the book and answer some of the questions about the material in bold letters in the chapters and do the questions at the back of the chapter."

"Do you do the homework?"

"A little, not much. I hand something in, he checks it off; he never looks at it, anyway."

"You have some science homework tonight?"

"Yeah, but I'm not going to do it."

"Did you bring the book home?"

"Yeah, I got it."

"Could we sit down together tonight and do it? I mean really do it and then come up with a question you could ask him about it. Like say, when I was doing it I got this idea and I want to ask you a question. Then we'll figure out a good question. Have you ever asked a question in that class?"

"He'd make fun of me."

"Maybe, but tell him you worked on it with your mother and she wants you to ask this question and come back and explain it to her. Be real nice about it. Tell him, if he'll answer it so you can understand it and explain it to her, she might help you again. It might not be exciting but it won't be as boring. If we can come up with a good question, I think it'll be interesting. Get the book, I'll help you. I can take an hour off from what I'm doing."

"But he'll expect me to do homework every day."

"Look, let's do it once and see what happens. If we figure out something good, you may have a day that's not so boring. I'm trying to help. If you've got a better idea, I'll go for it. I think it's also the student's job to do something so school's not so boring. Even if you don't want to do it, I'll bet you never thought about doing this. . . .

"So there you are, Kim. What do you think?"

"I don't think she'd do it."

"Is this your way of saying you don't want to try to do this with Jody?"

"But will I have to do this every day? I told you how busy I am. I don't have the time."

"Look, Kim. You don't have to do anything I suggest. You know that. Maybe just try it once. All I'm suggesting is that a parent who's worried about a kid like Jody has to connect with her to solve any problem. If you just sit around and worry, nothing's going to happen. The only alternative I can offer is do nothing and forget about her school problems. If you try to make her do anything, you're right back at square one."

Kim called me in a few days. What I suggested didn't work as well as I'd hoped but it got her and Jody talking about school. Most of all, it got Jody to realize that Kim wasn't going to make her do anything, but she'd help if Jody wanted. Over the next few weeks, Jody kept checking with Kim about school. She was testing whether Kim was going to try to make her do schoolwork. One day about a month later, four of Jody's girlfriends came over and wanted to talk with Kim about school. They wanted to know why Kim was so cool.

Kim explained a little choice theory to them. She told them she could only control her own behavior, she couldn't control Jody. She'd help Jody at home but that was all. Jody's work in school was up to her. If she were bored, if any of them were bored, what they did or didn't do was up to them. They had a long talk. The whole idea of parents getting off their backs about school was a new idea. Kim could feel them all getting close to her and she could see that Jody was noticing it. Kim told me she'd settle for Jody being close and not ruining her life at the parties. If Jody went to school, which she did, that was good enough. But Jody started doing a little more schoolwork—not enough to make much difference, but this way Kim figured she was holding her own. To try to get more would risk getting less.

I told her to keep in touch, to feel that I was there even if I couldn't really help her any more than I did. Jody never did much in school but she graduated. She got a job and that fall she enrolled in a junior college. I never heard any more. If things had gotten real bad, I'm sure I would have heard.

TWELVE

FRED

Because I'm reasonably well known, I occasionally get a client like Fred, an expensively dressed, take-over-the-conversation kind of man in his late forties. He started right in: "You have to help me. The lawyer handling my divorce told me you're the best there is and I never work with anyone but the best."

He paused and waited for my reaction. All I could come up with was, "Tell me why I'm so important."

"She's blackmailing me. She claims I'm a bad influence on my kids. She hardly lets them see me anymore. All she wants is more money and I need someone like you to say I deserve more time with them."

"Slow down a little, we've got plenty of time. Tell me, how many are there? How old are they?"

"There're three, all girls, thirteen, fifteen, and eighteen and—"

I interrupted, "They're old enough to make up their own minds; your wife can't keep them away from you if they want to see you."

"I know that. But she's poisoned them against me. She hates me and she's using them to get back at me. Since we divorced, and, God knows, I gave her everything I could afford in the settlement, I got into a sweet deal and made some real money. It was in the papers, she knows about it. She wants a million dollars. That's what this thing with the girls is all about."

"Have you talked this over with your daughters? What do they say?"

"They agree with her. They won't listen to my side of the story. They're still mad at me for leaving their mother. They saw how she treated me but they're still on her side."

"They can't be that mad at you. Okay. They see you, they talk with you. And if she's so mad at you, why do you think she doesn't try to stop them from seeing you altogether?"

"Oh, you don't know how smart she is. She encourages them to see me. She's got them convinced that they're the only ones who can get her the money she deserves. She's trying to get my own children to pick my pocket."

"Did you leave their mother for another woman?"

"What's that got to do with it? I want you to see the girls and convince them that I'm a good father. I pay all my child support. I want you to see my ex and convince her what she's doing is harming the girls. You're a psychiatrist, don't you think what she's doing is harming them? She's an unfit mother. I need you on my side. I'll pay whatever you want."

"Look, Fred, I know you're upset or I'd be a little angry at what you just said. I'm not a hired gun. I'm not on your side or your ex's side. If I'm on anyone's side, I'm on the girls' side. I try to be on all your sides in a situation like this. Even though you're divorced, whether you or your ex like it or not, you're still a family. If you still want me to get involved, I see my job as helping you as a family. Getting divorced doesn't make you any less the father or your ex any less the mother or the girls any less your children."

"That's what I'm talking about, I'm a good father and she's a lousy mother. I need you to say so."

"I think you need me to help all of you. I'm not here to

point a finger at anyone. If you don't agree, we're wasting time, yours and mine."

"Okay, if you mean her, too, not just me."

"Please, tell me her name; actually I'd like to know the girls' names, too. It's easier for me when I know names."

"My ex's name is Sandie; the oldest, that's the eighteen-year-old, is Julia; the fifteen-year-old is Lisa; and the baby, I mean the thirteen-year-old, is Kami."

"Good, that helps. I wonder, are you still with the woman you left your wife for? What's her name?

"Rhonda, and I'm not with her. That only lasted a year. Why do you want to know that?"

"Is there another woman in your life right now? If there is, she's part of the family and whatever I'm going to try to help you work out has to involve her. If she has children, yours or someone else's, they're part of the family, too."

"I come here with a simple request and you're making a federal case out of it. You want to know about my mother, too? She's hammering away at me about what's happening almost every day. She and Sandie's mother are very tight. They're both on my case. It's a mess."

"No, I don't need to know that much about the mothers but it goes to show how many people are involved. If you'd just tell me about any woman you're with now, it would help me get a better picture of the situation. I'm not looking to decide what's right or wrong, if that's what you're worried about. That's for all the people involved to decide, including the three girls. I'm not here to blame you for anything. I'm here to help people, not to look for fault."

"I left Sandie for a much younger woman six years ago after we were married seventeen years. I married the woman I left her for. I had to or she'd have left me and I thought she loved me. I sure figured her wrong. It lasted a year and we divorced. I'd gotten her to sign an ironclad prenup so I didn't have to pay much to lawyers but it still cost me a bundle. The girls hated her and they let her know it. Sandie wouldn't speak one word to me while I was with her. She hardly speaks to me now and only if it has to do with the girls."

"Are you with someone now?"

"Not really. I see a couple of women but I don't live with anyone. And believe me, I keep them totally separate from the girls. You can't believe how they hated Rhonda. It was frightening. The girls wanted me to go back to Sandie and they still do. But it wouldn't work even if she were interested, which she isn't."

He sighed and paused for a moment. Then he said, "I've really messed up my life."

I didn't know if he wanted me to say anything to that and I didn't know what to say so I didn't say anything. I paused for a moment, too, to show that I had some feeling for what he was suffering because, for all his bravado, Fred was a very unhappy man.

Then I said, "Okay, now that I have a good grasp of the situation, what do you see me doing?"

"Whatever you think'll help."

I appreciated his willingness to change his attitude and I tried to show my appreciation by changing my tone from a questioning to a problem-solving one. I said, "I think the first thing you should do is to try to get the money situation straightened out. It's casting a pall over anything we might try to work out. You were married to Sandie for seventeen years. You were married to . . ."

"Rhonda."

"To Rhonda for a year. You said you paid a bundle to settle your prenup. Who got more: Sandie or Rhonda?"

As you can see, the old Fred was still somewhat in the picture when he said, "I thought you were a psychiatrist not a lawyer. Where does that question fit in?"

I didn't pay any attention to that dig; it was kind of a reflex, and there was no real malice in his voice. I answered him by saying, "It comes from my concern for your children."

"But, I'm your client."

"Sure you are. And so are the rest of your family, Sandie and your three girls. They want me to find out if you treated them fairly when you left them."

"How do you know what they want?"

"If you were they, wouldn't you want to know the answer to that question? Don't be uncomfortable; you were in a tight situation when you left them, emotionally and financially. I'm not here to criticize you. That's another thing I don't do, criticize. From what you told me, the girls think you've cheated both them and their mother. If you want them back, I think you'll have to deal with that situation."

"Rhonda got more, a lot more, but the idea of giving Sandie a lot of money . . . I mean, you don't know how she treated me for years."

I interrupted. The last thing I wanted to do was get involved with that marriage, actually with either of his marriages. I said, "Fred, I know you left your wife because you were unhappy with her. I don't expect you to start liking her now any more than I expect her to start thinking well of you. I'm not a marriage counselor trying to resurrect your marriage. But your family's split apart. That's what brought you into my office. I'm trying to help you get it back together even if you and Sandie are split. The girls need both of you no matter how you feel about each other. I'm hoping that both of you love them enough so you'll make the effort for this to happen."

"You know I love my daughters; that's what brought me in here."

"Do you think Sandie loves them?"

"Of course she loves them, we both love them."

"Do Sandie or the girls know how much money you gave that woman?"

"She lied to them."

"Who lied to them?"

"Rhonda, the bitch who got the prenup, told my daughters I gave her a million. That's why Sandie is asking for a million. I told the girls it was only half a million but no one believes me."

"You have no proof?"

"It was cash, the prenup called for cash; don't ask me for the details of that deal. I gave her the half mil."

"Do the girls think you can afford a million? Do they have any idea what you're worth? You know what you made on the sweet deal you mentioned."

"I could afford a million. I just hate giving any of it to Sandie. Besides, it's blackmail, where will it stop?"

"Look, you handle the money. Do what you want. But what I want to help you with is your girls and geting along better with Sandie. But when I say help you, I mean just you. I have no intention of seeing any of them. I think you'd be wise not to bring me into the picture, but if they ask if you're getting help or advice, tell them the truth. I'm helping you to be a better father and to get along better with their mother, something like that."

"Okay, that makes sense. My girls are in pretty good shape. They don't need counseling right now. Their mother does, but she can find one on her own like I did. What do we do now?"

"Tell me about your girls. You say they're in pretty good shape."

"The young ones are fine. They were little and the divorce didn't hit them so hard but the eighteen-year-old, Julia, she's almost nineteen, she was twelve and very close to her mother.

She still is, she was really upset. She seems okay now but I worry about her."

"That's been my experience. Divorce, especially when one of the parents walks out on the other, is very hard for teenagers to accept and twelve is in that range. Even children in their twenties take it very hard. I think you have good reason to worry about her. How's she doing in school? Is she in college?"

"She does great in school. She worked hard for a scholarship and she got one. She doesn't want to take money from me. She makes remarks like, 'Give Mom the money, she needs it more than I do.' She's at UCLA now but she still lives at home. It's her social life that worries me. For a long time she stayed away from boys, but last year, when she was in the twelfth grade, she started going with a college junior. They got into it pretty heavy, I mean sexually, everything. She started talking about marriage and it got too scary for him and he dropped her. She handled it but I could see she was upset. I tried to talk with her but she laughed at me and said, 'What do you know about love?' Now in college she's mentioned a teaching assistant she met. He's almost thirty. I'm happy she's told me about him, at least she trusts me that much, but I don't know what to say so I just keep my mouth shut. I've tried to talk to Sandie about it but she yelled at me and said, 'With you for a role model, what do you expect?' I want to be a good father but I don't seem to know how. When we get together, I take them shopping. The younger girls like it but Julia sees through it. She only buys things because it makes her sisters happy. A lot of the stuff she takes back. Her sisters tell me."

"What do you do with them when they see you? You must do something more than take them shopping."

"That's the point, they're teenage girls. I don't know what to do with them when they come. It's awkward. When I married

Rhonda, I thought she'd help but that was a disaster. One of the women I see now is a high school teacher. I've talked to her about it and she said she'd help. But I'm afraid to get her involved. I mean I'm not in love with her and I don't think I ever want to get married again. What in the world does a father like me do with three teenage girls without their mother?"

"I haven't a good answer for that question but I'd like to talk to you about what I think you should do next. If you're able to do it, then I think we may be able to get the girls to help you with that problem. It's as much their problem as yours, maybe more. When are you going to see all three of the girls again?"

"This weekend. That's why I was so anxious to see you this week."

"Are they comfortable at your place? Do they accept it as a place they like to come to?"

"It's a real nice condo. Three bedrooms, the other two are all fixed up for them. I was smart, I let them pick out a lot of the stuff in the whole place. They went with me when I worked with the decorator. I had a fancier condo but I had to sell it to get the money to pay Rhonda off. But it was okay. They'd made it clear that they'd wanted me to get rid of anything to do with Rhonda."

"That's good. What I'd like you to do is talk with them. Tell them you love them but you're not going back to their mother. Ask them what they'd like you to do with them, how you should treat them, to tell you anything on their mind. Tell them that they are never going to have another father or another mother even if either you or Sandie remarry. Tell them what I said about your being a family even if you and Sandie are divorced. Listen to all they have to say but also help them out on the money issue. I'm not telling you what to do but it's an issue you're going to have to face. Do you think you can do it? And one more thing. Ask them if they'd be willing to have you make a tape of your conversation so, if they wanted, they could play it for their mother."

"Up until you mentioned the tape, I was with you. But that woman really doesn't like me. I'm worried about that."

"The tape is to show her you want to be up front and let her know you're still a family. Anything that concerns them concerns both you and their mother. Right now they're all on Sandie's side, especially Julia. If you're easy to talk with, this'll kind of balance your situation. But be careful, don't say anything to them that'd make anything worse for you or for Sandie. You make deals, this is a big deal. I wish I could be sitting in your ear to advise you but I'm going to give you something to read that ought to help. Read it carefully and then call me if you have questions."

I gave him the material from the first two chapters of this book. Anyone who reads this will have read that. It's clear and usable and I believed it would help him.

"Do you think I'm ready to do this? I don't want to screw it up."

"If you pay attention to what I gave you to read, I think you'll be ready to do this. It has to be done and the sooner the better. You have to behave in a way that the girls see you as an important part of their life. You have to be very careful not to say anything against Sandie, not a single word."

"That'll mean I have to come up with some money. I've taken some big hits in the market."

"Fred, whose responsibility is your family? Figure out the money problem. I have a lot of faith you can handle it. Read the stuff I gave you."

"I'll read it as soon as I get home. Can I call you tonight?"

"Sure, I'll leave a message for my service to connect you as soon as you tell them who you are."

"You sure this is a good idea?"

"Are you sure of every deal you go into?"

"I'll talk to you tonight before ten."

A little past nine the phone rang and it was Fred. As soon as I said hello, he started in. "That stuff you gave me about external control, the deadly habits, the criticizing, the complaining, the blaming, the nagging; my God, there it all was. Our marriage didn't have a chance. Sandie was bad, Rhonda was worse."

"How about Fred? You didn't mention Fred's part in what happened to the marriages."

"I didn't think I had to mention my part. Do you really want to hear all the gory details?"

"I'm sorry, Fred. No, I don't. Just your telling me gives me a lot of hope for your meeting with the girls."

"I've double underlined what I think is the most important thing in what you gave me. It was that part about all we do is behave and we choose all our behavior. But the biggie is that everything we say should keep us close or get us closer. And then when you claimed that before we say it, we know if that's going to happen and we should keep our mouths shut. I kept remembering me saying to you when I was ranting about Sandie, 'I'll pay you whatever you want.' I knew you'd be upset by that but I said it anyway. It's a miracle you didn't throw me out of your office."

"You feel better about your talk with the girls?"

"I can handle it. I'll be okay. I'm thinking about it and I'll be ready. I'm working on how I'm going to start it. If I can get it off to a good start, it'll be okay."

We talked for another fifteen minutes or I should say he

talked. Mostly I just listened and sent the message with my silence that I had faith in him. He and Sandie had seventeen years of the deadly habits. He really got it. I felt a lot better. I was looking forward to seeing him after his meeting with the girls.

THIRTEEN

The School Counselor as a Surrogate Parent

In chapter 5, I described how two school counselors arranged for a responsible high school student to work with a middle school student who had no parents and only an overwhelmed grandma, to make friends with him and try to get him connected. In this chapter I will let my wife, Carleen, describe what she did for twelve years as a high school counselor in a small school district in Ohio. Working with hundreds of students, she saw her job as giving the students the love and the guidance they needed at school as well as at home.

I CONSIDERED MYSELF lucky to be working in a school district whose superintendent had the foresight to create my job. It was 1983 and I had just completed my certification in school counseling, but in my school district where I had been employed as a teacher for thirteen years, there were no openings for a counselor. The district was small with only three elementary schools, one middle school, and one high school. The middle school had one male and one female counselor and so did the high school. That seemed to be tradition. It had been that way for years.

Not really wanting to seek employment elsewhere, I

decided to ask the superintendent if he would consider adding me to the counseling staff half-time, serving the three elementary schools, and half-time as the district's drug and alcohol prevention program coordinator. This would include having an office at the high school where I was already a teacher and where I could create a group counseling room. I wanted to help students who had problems and start a leadership training and peer counseling project for interested high school students.

The community in which the schools were located had quite unique demographics, part blue-collar, part welfare recipients, mostly Caucasian, and 10 percent African American whose numbers were split just about evenly between the two socioeconomic groups. There was an unusually high incidence of alcoholism and drug abuse in all groups. Since the people lived in three small villages and a sprawling area that could be described as suburban-rural, the crime rate was lower than in the inner city. The most frequent disturbances were domestic violence and drunk driving.

Our students were the recipients and often the pitiful victims of the neglect and abuse accompanying these problems in the community and home. Apparently, the superintendent convinced the school board without too much difficulty to accept my proposal. Either they thought it was a good idea that was much needed or they thought if I was willing to assume such an undertaking, I ought to have a chance to try.

My first year as the district counselor was spent running from one elementary school to the next putting emotional Band-Aids on children who never seemed to stop bleeding, and there was an endless supply of them. I remember a fifth grade boy one day whose face was so swollen he couldn't open his eyes. His father had punched him repeatedly in the face for not obeying him. We got the children's protective agency to come out, take pictures, remove the child from the home, only to be returned a week later because . . . I didn't know why. All I knew was we now had a very angry father on our hands who belonged to a motorcycle gang and lived near the school. The boy survived, we survived, and he eventually graduated high school in the vocational program, but he never lost his anger. So many never would.

But I was lucky to be there because I believed I could figure out how to help them help themselves and each other. That's when I started group guidance-on-a-cart at each elementary school. That is, I spent thirty minutes a week in every classroom in all three schools doing kindergarten through fifth grade guidance activities. I believed guidance was for every student, not just a few.

Again, I was lucky to work for a superintendent and principals who saw the value of in-service training and paid for me to attend workshops at the Center for Reality Therapy in Cincinnati, the Council on Alcoholism, and various programs sponsored by local treatment facilities for adolescent drug and alcohol problems. These were invaluable to me and I used the skills I learned every day.

In every classroom I started teaching children about safety and about ways to get along better with each other as well as how to help one another solve problems and get their needs met without hurting themselves or others.

In the kindergarten I read stories and sang songs with them. A half hour there was about all I could handle. I asked those teachers how on earth they could do this all day long. It's like working in a bucket of worms; kindergartners are kinetic!

Back at the high school I was working almost every afternoon with three to four groups of drug-recovering and alcohol-dependent students, children of alcoholics, or those having other problems, and with one leadership training group. The purpose of the leadership group was to identify nontraditional leaders in the school who would work as volunteer peer counselors and do community service.

My job as drug prevention program coordinator included a community outreach component. At that time, the Nancy Reagan Chemical People Task Force concept was being promoted nationwide and I was ready to become involved by representing our district. With the help of many people—leaders in the community, parents, teachers, administrators, and board of education members—we organized a town meeting at the most centrally located village town hall. It was right before the November elections and everybody who was anybody, and then some, showed up. It was so politically correct and well publicized that no one could afford not to come. We showed the Nancy Reagan video on the new larger-than-life television screens someone had arranged for us to borrow. The local cable network was there to cover it. There was standing room only.

I had asked some of the parents of recovering adolescents to speak, and their plea to the community to do something about this problem had an impact few could imagine. The result was far-reaching. A community task force was immediately set up and we began meeting every other week to plan programs for parents and get help for students who needed it.

Being in an isolated area in southwestern Ohio, residents had few resources, fewer services, and no public transportation to take them to those services. It was arranged somehow that I would be invited to become a member of the County Mental Health Board of Directors for our catchment area. That way I could have direct access to information about how we might get a satellite drug counselor set up near the high school.

The church across the street from the school provided free space and within a few months we had a licensed alcoholism counselor to serve the whole community during the school day and some evenings. We figured if the people could get to the high school for football and basketball games (which, by the way, were the only show in town), they could get to our counselor. High school students with substance abuse problems could leave school for an hour and go right across the street. The counselor also worked part-time in a makeshift office that was in the same town hall used for the Chemical People meeting.

Using the federally funded drug-free moneys for prevention programs, we provided each school with age-appropriate curriculum materials and teacher in-service training to supplement our efforts. Everyone became just more aware of what to look for.

I was so lucky to have the parents and community leaders from the task force behind all my efforts. They not only supported everything we were trying to do in the schools, they became actively involved and it made a difference.

One group volunteered to take turns driving recovering students back to their treatment center across town to attend AA meetings. They would never have been able to get there on their own and would have relapsed as in the past. The encouragement these adults provided and the nonjudgmental interactions they had with these students on the way to and from the meetings were just as helpful as the meetings themselves. The students made some life-saving connections and many, for the first time in their young lives, began to trust and respect adults.

Another way these wonderful people helped was to

cofacilitate the high school support groups with me. They came to share their wisdom, but mostly they just came, and accepted and loved these teenagers who needed them so much. Drugs, alcohol, violence, and deception had nearly destroyed their young lives, and the connections they made in these groups began to turn their lives around.

What we did in these groups with the students was different from anything they had ever experienced. After hearing each of them tell their "horror story," the next question we asked each student was, "What could you do today to get closer to someone who really matters to you?" We never talked about their drug or alcohol use. We only talked about what they could do to build better relationships in their lives.

Together they made the decision to help one another in school first. Walking down the hall one day, I saw one of my groupies give the other a wink as if to say, "I'm here for you if you need me." The wink was returned with a big smile. The support group was working.

This is just an overview of my days as a district counselor. I held that position for six years. Then the principals decided they would like to have a full-time elementary counselor, and at the same time the one male counselor at the high school was going to take the job of athletic director the following school year. I had a choice to make.

I took the high school counseling position, breaking with the district's longtime tradition of a male boys' counselor and a female girls' counselor. The other female counselor and I were responsible for all the scheduling, testing, credits, and applications for college and scholarships. She took care of students whose names began with A through L and I had M through Z. There was lots of paperwork but no more traveling from school to school in all kinds of weather, which was a little piece of heaven. I had maintained my large group counseling room for my office, which was carpeted, wood paneled, and had twenty upholstered stacking chairs to put in a circle for groups.

My biggest frustration was that I had so much paperwork to do I barely had time to see students. I managed to keep up my groups and do some individual counseling only because my colleague, who really knew the ropes, helped me beyond belief. She understood what I was trying to do with the kids and being an excellent counselor, she extended herself in every way. We actually became quite a team seeing any student who needed us, no matter what letter of the alphabet his or her name began with.

Eventually I learned to speed up the performance of my paper-chase duties and with extra help from capable student volunteers on anything that wasn't confidential information, I had more time to help troubled students and run groups.

Being at the high school all day had many advantages. I was able to groom a network of students who would come and tell me if someone in the school needed help. We worked together to get them in to see me. That's where the peer counseling training paid off.

Early one day, near Thanksgiving, one of my kids came to me and said I'd better see Glen, a popular senior. He'd been acting strange and had told one of his friends he didn't have anything to live for. He'd found out his girlfriend had been cheating on him and he had rifles in his house. This was a community of hunters and almost every family owned guns.

Instead of sending for Glen, I went looking for him. He was in government class so I asked his teacher if I could borrow him for a while. He said simply, "Glen you're needed in the office." I took him to my office where I had assembled a couple of his buddies.

When he walked into the room and saw them sitting there, at first he got angry, then he started to cry. They got up and put their arms around his shoulders and sat him down. They talked all afternoon. We found out he was very hurt, but he wasn't going to kill himself over her. I asked Glen if we could call his mom and tell her what was going on. He looked embarrassed but relieved to get it off his chest. She came immediately from work and picked him up from my office. We all talked; they hugged and went home feeling closer than they had felt in a long time.

That one had a happy ending. The following year the family of another young man had to endure the worst kind of tragedy. It was only weeks before the event that we had called his parents, who were prominent community members, to tell them we were concerned about their son's behavior. As a result of several incidents where alcohol was involved, his name kept coming up. The parents were bewildered and somewhat in denial and we backed off.

Then it happened. As far as anyone could determine, Joel had been drinking heavily since school let out Friday afternoon. He had also been fighting with his girlfriend all week. By early Saturday, around three or four in the morning, he returned home and picked up a gun. Shots were fired and by dawn Joel was dead. No one knew exactly what had happened. On Monday, we had a school full of grieving students. Joel was a senior and had been on the football team, and was well liked by everyone. All we as counselors could do in the school was try to comfort and offer counseling to anyone who wanted it, including the teachers, who were devastated.

The next day a whole group of seniors were in the

school library just sitting around staring at each other. I walked in and started talking to a few of them who looked as if they were in shock, eyes all red and swollen. I asked them a question that at the time probably seemed insane. "So, what can you do right now that might help?" They looked at me as if I'd lost my mind. Then one girl stood up and said, "Let's make something to help us remember Joel." Somebody asked, "What do you mean?" Someone else said, "Yeah, let's get his jersey from the coach and pictures from the yearbook advisor."

The momentum picked up and before I knew it everyone was getting up with a purpose. They were determined to do something and the result was a beautiful memory space in the front hall display case. It helped them grieve his loss. That spring, a tree was planted on the front lawn of the school. His favorite teacher silently took care of that tree for years, long after all of Joel's classmates had graduated and moved on.

I started a group that year Joel died for students grieving the loss of a loved one, and Joel's younger brother attended until he graduated. The lesson we all learned from that tragedy was to reach out to one another before it's too late.

We had some difficult girls in the school who wouldn't hesitate to "kick butt" at the slightest provocation. Feuds would start in the neighborhood and be carried to school like some contagious disease. Often, the principal would recruit me to intervene. Girl fights are the worst nightmare for a school counselor. One such fight had been going on for days and every time I talked to the girls they'd promise to work it out peacefully.

Finally, after their promises had been broken once too often, I tried a different tack. I told their parents what I was trying to do and asked them if they would help by coming in for a conference with the girls present. They said they would come and then I began to worry. What was I getting myself into?

It could have become a free-for-all, but because I started the meeting by asking each one what they would be willing to do personally to help solve the problem, we somehow got off on the right foot. One of the fathers began by saying he'd be willing to take all the girls to Hamburger Heaven for supper tonight so they could talk about being friends again on a full stomach. That got a laugh and the ice was broken. Of course, his daughter was mortified, but the rest of the ice maidens were charmed.

After that meeting, the girls became almost best friends again. That's when I asked them to join the leadership training group. I figured, why let all that energy go untapped? They could put it to work doing something constructive.

This brings me to the part I enjoy telling the most. My leadership groups attracted a lot of unusual students. By that, I mean they were not the most popular kids in the school; nor were they leaders in the traditional sense. For instance, they seldom ran for office and they rarely belonged to any organizations. They weren't the best students or the best athletes. They were just kids who didn't have a mission yet, but they had lots of opinions. They mostly found fault with everybody and complained about everything.

I would continually ask them, "So, what are you going to do about that?" I'll tell you, they did a lot in the first four years I worked with them. Individual groups met whenever they had a common study hall, and all the groups met together after school once a month.

The main complaint I heard was that there was no place for them to go at night to have fun that was legal. What they did about that was just short of amazing. Their plan was to start a teen canteen. They began by meeting with the village council to testify, stating their needs and making an appeal. They made appointments with various adults in the community, like the Kiwanis and Jaycees, to discuss funding for the project. They even met with the chief of police to discuss lifting the curfew on canteen nights.

After numerous meetings and endless phone calls, they finally got permission to use the town hall. They hired a young man they liked who drove a school bus for the district, and his wife, to be permanent, on-site managers. Opening night they had a dance, which drew over three hundred teenagers and ended without one incident. There were four or five parents and a paid security guard on hand, but they just stood around and watched the kids have fun.

When teenagers want to do something, there is no limit to how much they can accomplish and "Teen Turf" was but one example of their capability, determination, and commitment to an idea. A caring community of cooperative adults doesn't hurt either.

Another project grew out of yet one more problem. The kids complained, "We can't even go to the library in town without all those old fogies yelling at us. If we stand around outside talking, they call the cops. They hate all teenagers." My question again was, "So, what are you going to do about it?" It was met with groans and excuses. They didn't know what to do. They felt helpless. The new Senior Citizens Center was housed in the same building as the brand-new public library in the village with the now famous town hall. The village had a lot of money invested in this center and library.

Teenagers and senior citizens have essentially the same problem: A lot of people are prejudiced against them. They also see each other as a threat and are suspicious of one another. I called the director of the Senior Center and invited him to be a guest speaker at our next after-school meeting of the combined leadership groups. He came and after his talk the kids were all over him with their questions. After answering them all, he presented them with an idea that got them thinking. He asked if they had ever thought about adopting a grandparent.

They laughed, but I said, "Maybe we could invite them here, like on a sign-up basis, one grandparent per student."

Someone else said, "Yeah, we could have lunch and take them to our classes." Now they were thinking. "We could get tape recorders and interview them about what life was like when they were our age."

I said, "Someday, you might even tape what's called a living history, sort of the story of their life, and give it to them to leave to their own children."

All of that actually did happen, and so much more. The teens really made connections with quite a few of those lively and spirited senior citizens. It was hard to distinguish who was having the most fun at their gatherings. They invited the students who adopted them back to the hallowed halls of the center to have lunch (with homemade desserts, a big hit). They sang songs and learned how to dance to each other's music. There were a couple of pool tables there and I don't know who was snookering whom, but they enjoyed playing together. The end result was the misunderstandings and complaints about one another stopped and were replaced with some genuine warm feelings and lasting friendships.

I can't stress enough how important my parent and grandparent connection was to the success of everything I was doing with the students. The projects for which I most appreciated parents' participation were those involving overnight retreats.

When you are responsible for teenage boys and girls together for any reason, anywhere, overnight, it's a challenge. I was lucky to have so much cooperation from the parents I asked to help me. We pulled it off with hundreds of students over the years without a glitch. I believe we were successful because we were all able to talk openly. We trusted one another. We had taken the time to build a healthy relationship with each teen so that they saw us as adults who were looking out for them, not out to get them.

I believe it is crucial in light of the recent incidents of violence in our schools that a special person be available in the school at all times whom students can count on. Someone they can trust who will provide a safe place, a hot line, a network of caring people for every student to access and get help for himself/herself or for some other student.

If you as a parent of a teenager can spare any time, no matter how little, to volunteer as a counselor's helper, group cofacilitator, or community resource person, please do. It will be one of the most rewarding experiences you will ever have.

Teenagers are resilient but delicate works-in-progress. We can never love them too much. I have been continually amazed at the good they are capable of doing when given a place where they feel loved, have choices, and experience success, as well as the harm they are capable of doing when they are not. I consider myself lucky to have had the opportunity over the years to be there for so many of them. That was beyond luck; the experience, for me, was one of life's gifts.

There are countless dedicated teachers and counselors working in high schools all over who make a difference in young people's lives. Recently I met one in the Northeast whose work is inspiring and a great example of what this chapter is trying to convey.

Jon Erwin was an English teacher when he completed the training in choice theory. He is now an instructor for the William Glasser Institute and a staff development specialist for BOCES near Corning, New York. I have asked Jon to tell his story here.

AS AN ENGLISH TEACHER, I started teaching choice theory to my students to build a community in the classroom, to learn more about my students (and vice versa), to provide them with meaningful writing, speaking, and listening activities, and to help them understand literature. As the years went by, when students who had graduated called, wrote, or came back to visit, they sometimes thanked me for teaching them how to write or for exposing them to certain books, but almost without fail they told me how much choice theory had helped them in their lives.

When I took my present job as a staff development specialist at BOCES, I was no longer working directly with kids; my job is to teach teachers. Just by chance and because of child care difficulties, my son Nathan came to a couple of my after-school workshops. At one of them, I asked him if he would play a client in a role-play demonstration. The enthusiastic feedback I got from the participants affirmed an idea I had been thinking about for some time: the Choice Players, kids demonstrating and teaching the ideas of choice theory. It would give me the opportunity to work with kids again, teaching them what Dr. Glasser would call a-educational knowledge, useful knowledge and skills that can be improved throughout their lives. Also, the Choice Players would add a significant amount of credibility to my presentations.

Next, I needed a funding source. I found out about a local mini-grant from the Chemung County Office of Mental Health, applied for it, and received $1,000, which was more than enough to pay for materials, lunches, and transportation for the first Choice Players training. I then led a management presentation for a local youth leadership group called Young Leadership Chemung. At the end of the presentation I offered the Choice Player training to the group. Thirty-seven students expressed interest. By the time the training was held a few months later, eight were still interested, but they were eight highly motivated kids. Some other students found out about the training from parents or friends of their parents who had taken my Quality Classroom workshop or one of the Glasser Basic Intensive Weeks offered at BOCES. I ended up with twelve students for the first training. We had seven girls and five boys, ranging in age from ten to seventeen years old. We spent three full days during the summer, bonding as a team and learning about choice theory and reality therapy. The kids thoroughly enjoyed working together and learning what they immediately recognized as extremely valuable information.

That fall we met a couple more times preparing for what was our first major presentation, a workshop at the Quality Schools Consortium Conference in Boston. Dr. Glasser interviewed the students on stage in front of approximately five hundred educators and right afterward, we did our workshop entitled Students of Choice: How and Why to Teach Choice Theory to Kids. We had standing room only, and the kids did a marvelous job.

Since then we have expanded our membership to thirty students, who come from six different Choice Players chapters in six different school districts. We have a great deal of diversity within the group: kids from urban, suburban and rural schools; different ethnic backgrounds; different socioeconomic backgrounds; kids who have had lots of success in traditional school settings and students who have not. When we work together, though, they are just kids with a common vision and a common mission: to create a better world, one choice at a time.

Also since Boston, we have conducted workshops for local faculty meetings, school district conference days, and other local educational gatherings, as well as two Northeast regional conferences.

We have expanded the scope of our workshops to include:

Character by Choice: a choice theory approach to character development

The Solving Circle: designed to teach Dr. Glasser's structured reality therapy and the idea of the solving circle to resolve problems in relationships

Stress Less: a stress-reduction workshop for kids, focusing on Dr. Glasser's concept of total behavior

Students of Choice: This is the original workshop designed to help educators understand the benefits of teaching choice theory to kids, also providing them with fun, hands-on strategies for engaging kids in learning the ideas.

All of the Choice Players give powerful testimonials about how learning choice theory has helped them in their lives, particularly in their relationships with their parents and siblings.

FUTURE:

ONE of our next steps is to expand our membership. In each of our present schools, we have teachers or counselors who are trained and who act as the Choice Players' advisors. We hope to add more schools to our membership.

In the next month or two, we will be doing our first parent workshop with the parents of our current members. This summer we hope to create a video. We will continue to expand the scope of our workshops. Besides the parent workshop, we'd like to develop a workshop based on the ideas in the book *The Language of Choice Theory.* It seems to me that if we can teach people choice theory when they're young, before they've been immersed in external control psychology too long, there is a greater likelihood that they will live the ideas.

I think the Choice Players is an excellent way for teenagers to learn by teaching and to take ownership of their own and their community's growth and well-being. It is also a wonderful opportunity for adults to volunteer in a worthwhile adventure.

FOURTEEN

TERI AND STARR REVISITED

TERI

About a week after I saw Teri, I decided I'd call her parents and ask them to come in. I didn't ask them about how she'd been or anything about her behavior. I'd left Teri with the idea that she shouldn't automatically reject what her parents wanted her to do if it also benefited her. She admitted that this was working for her sister but she didn't want to accept any of their control no matter how it might benefit her. I also remembered that she did ask for one thing and that's all I wanted to talk about with them. Past that, anything that went on during their second visit would be up to them.

When they came in, I started with saying, "I enjoyed meeting Teri and we got on very well. I look forward to seeing her again."

Roger said, "You enjoyed talking to Teri?"

"She actually talked with you?" Susan added.

---

*NOTE: Teri was introduced in chapter 6, Starr in chapter 8.

"No problem, everyone talks with me and mostly we both enjoy it. It's been my experience that crazy people talk sane with me, depressed people cheer up with me. All the people who come here are unhappy. They like to talk to psychiatrists as long as we don't tell them what to do. As soon as you start telling a teenager what to do, she stops listening."

"But what we tell her is for her own good. You expect us to just sit there and watch her go down the drain?" Susan enjoyed telling me how to be a better psychiatrist.

"If they don't seem to see that what they're doing isn't good for them, I get around to it. But once they feel I accept them as they are, they get around to it themselves. Teri's moving in that direction. If she felt you and Roger accepted her, she'd talk to both of you."

"If she even came close to doing what we want her to, we'd accept her completely."

"Like we accept her sister," Roger added.

"I'm sure you would but that's not the problem, is it?"

"Are you asking us to accept her the way she acts, the way she goofs off in school, the way she dresses and wears her hair?" Susan said this as if the idea of anyone accepting Teri the way she was was beyond her ability to conceive.

"I'm not asking you to accept her. But you can make my job a lot easier if you'll do just one small thing. If you'd do it, I think I could help her in a few sessions. As I said, we seem to get along."

"What do you want us to do?" asked Roger. The fact that I was not going to ask for very much caught his attention.

Susan looked at me, waiting for my answer.

I said, "I'd like you to stop talking to her about school. I mean don't say a word or even give her a look if it sends a school message. That's all, nothing else. Could you do it?"

There was a pause. Each of them started to say something

but then each stopped. They looked at me and then they looked at each other. There must have been a half minute of silence. Finally I broke in by asking, "Are you considering it?"

"I can't speak for Roger but are you serious?"

"Susan, I hate answering a question with a question but why wouldn't I be serious?"

Roger said, "Because school is all we ever worry about. The other things are important but school's the critical issue."

"I'm not asking you to stop worrying about it. All I'm asking is you don't talk to Teri about it. I'm not joking. I'm dead serious."

"But what'll happen to her schoolwork?" asked Susan.

"It'll either stay the same or it'll get better. It won't get any worse."

Roger must have been a businessman. He said, "Can you guarantee that?"

"Money back. No charge for seeing her if her schoolwork gets worse. I have no hesitation at all in guaranteeing that. Teri wants it, and considering how much she hates being nagged about school, she's still doing passing work. She has no reason to do worse. I'll also tell her that I asked you to both do it and that will increase my credibility."

Also, because I was a little frustrated by all their external control, I said jokingly, "I'll make you a better deal if you want. I'll refund double what you'd pay me if her schoolwork goes down if you'll pay me double if it goes up. You don't get a deal like that very often from a doctor."

Susan said, "But how can you be so sure?"

"Because Teri told me she's going to graduate even with all your bugging. If you get off her back about school, I'm betting she'll put some of the energy she's using to resist you into her schoolwork. I'd say the odds are more than ten to one in my favor. But you've got to do it. If you slip, apologize right away."

They kept looking at each other and then back at me. I said, "Do we have a deal?"

Roger said, "If we stop bugging her about school, maybe we should stop bugging her about all the other stuff."

"I'd be all for it. The way I see it, the less you bug the more you get. And look at the bright side. If this doesn't work, you can blame me. It's awful to have no one to blame when things don't work out."

I laid it on pretty thick but I was asking a lot of Susan and Roger and I thought lightening things up would be okay. They felt good when they left the office. It was almost as if I'd taken a load off their backs, which in a sense, I think I had. I had the feeling that they might actually do more than I suggested. I was glad for Teri.

Sure enough, the next time she came she started right in, "My parents have changed. It's weird. What did you do to them?"

"I told them the truth. I told them that we got along real well and they didn't believe me."

"I didn't think we got along that well."

"You're back. And I don't think you made fun of me to your girlfriends like you planned, did you?"

"How did you know that?"

"I see a lot of teenage girls."

"I guess you do. Anyway when I told my girlfriends what you said, like I shouldn't screw up my life by resisting the nice things my parents want to do for me, they thought that was good advice. I'd just gotten to the point where I thought all they wanted was to make my life miserable. Do you think they're off my back permanently?"

"I think that's pretty much up to you."

"What do you mean?"

"I mean if you'll talk to them just like you're talking to me,

I think things'll stay this way. Tell them you want their opinion, you just don't want them to bug you if you don't agree. Talk it over with your sister. She's been doing something like that for years."

"Do I have to keep seeing you?"

"I think it'd be a good idea. It would reassure your folks that you have someone and they don't have to feel you're all on your own. But when you come, feel free to bring your girlfriends once in a while. All teenagers can use what I'm trying to teach you and then you won't have to tell them what we talked about."

She looked at me with a little more interest and said, "What exactly are you trying to teach me?"

"It's called choice theory. It's a theory that says we choose all we do. The better the choices you make, the happier you are. Like making some better choices about how you deal with your folks. Like when you said your folks were out to make your life miserable. That was a bad choice. If everything you do is a choice, then it helps if you know how to make good choices."

"But how will I know what's a good choice?"

"You know because you feel it. Have you ever said something to one of your girlfriends and she got mad at you for a while?"

"All the time. Just today, I told Stephanie that her hair was too long and she really got pissed. She didn't talk to me for the rest of the day. As soon as I get home, I'm going to call her and apologize. It was a stupid thing to say."

"Did you have any idea before you said it that it was stupid, that she'd get pissed at you?"

"But it is too long."

"Says who?"

"Okay, I get it."

"You may be right but you made a bad choice by saying it.

And even before you said it, you got a little feeling that it might be a bad thing to say but since you were so sure you were right, you said it anyway."

"I do that all the time. Things I shouldn't say keep popping out of my mouth. You should hear me at home."

"Do things like that keep popping out of your sister's mouth?"

"No."

"Do you think she never thinks things like that?"

"When we talk she tells me things I don't even think of saying to my folks."

"So she chooses to keep her mouth shut and you don't. She makes better choices than you make. She knows choice theory and you don't. Hasn't she been trying to teach you all along what I've just explained?"

"But you're different."

"Of course I'm different. People who know choice theory are a lot different. You're learning it; you're different from what you were last week. I think you're better off."

"Maybe. But I could go right back to the way I was."

"You could choose to go right back to the way you were. And when you do, you'll feel worse than you do now. If you keep seeing me, we'll talk a lot about the choices you're thinking about and which ones to make and which not to make. In a few weeks I can teach you a lot about feeling better. And your friends, too. We'll talk to Stephanie; she'll remember what you said about her hair. She might want to learn what she could have said that would have saved both of you a lot of upset. When you learn choice theory, you begin to get along a lot better with everyone and you don't have to give in, either. Does your sister give in that much to your parents?"

"They give in to her, I told you about that new Mustang."

We went on to talk about a lot of the bad choices she'd been making recently. And how she could have made better choices. I saw her on a regular basis for about a year. But I saw her folks and taught them a lot of choice theory, too. Wouldn't it be a wonderful world if schools taught kids and parents choice theory? It's easy to do because, like Teri, both kids and parents like to learn this new way to relate to the people in their lives.

I know you may be saying to yourself that every kid can't have access to a counselor or to choice theory in school. But both teens and parents can learn a lot of choice theory by reading this book and some of the other books listed in appendix A.

STARR

Ed and Sara kept in close touch with me and with the clinic staff who were dealing directly with Starr. I told them that I did not want to have any personal contact with her. It would be confusing to her. I would only counsel them about what they should do with Starr at home and I would be more than happy to tell the clinic staff what I was doing with them.

It only took a few days for Starr to realize that things at home were different. Following my advice, Ed and Sara changed but did not make a big deal about what they were now doing. They told Starr that if she wanted anything special, her mother would cook it for her or she could buy her own food and cook it herself. But that was all. I explained the choice theory to them as I had explained it to Teri's parents and they were now going to choose to stop saying any more about food or how Starr ate or didn't eat it.

What they couldn't help noticing was that Starr was eating more of her mother's cooking now that she had the option to buy her own food and cook it herself. Basically, as long as she felt she had choices, she didn't have to make an effort to refuse her mother's food because her mother was no longer watching what she was eating. Of course, she tested. She'd skip a meal. Or make a big deal out of saying she wouldn't eat what Sara had prepared as if to challenge Sara's new way of not trying to make her eat. When she did this, Sara would tell her that she was free to do what she wanted about eating.

Ed and Sara also tried to get her more involved with other teenage girls, to encourage her to connect with a girl her own age. They may have referred to her doing this differently but they were careful to watch her face. If she frowned or rolled her eyes at what they were suggesting, they cut it off immediately. Even when Starr went out of her way to get them to revert to any of their former external control behaviors so that she'd have something to resist and blame them for, they abstained. They were better at it than Roger and Susan, but they had a much more serious problem to motivate them to change from external control to choice theory.

Because Starr was involved with a group at the clinic, Sara asked her if she'd met anyone there she liked. At first she pooh-poohed Sara's suggestion, but Sara noticed that she did not really resist, so she mentioned a couple of times that she was free to invite a friend for a night or a weekend. When she finally invited a girl named Janet for the weekend, the girls had a good time. Janet was surprised that the subject of food or eating was, if you'll excuse me, off the table at their house.

Starr told a surprised Janet that if they wanted to make their own food, they could go shopping for it and cook it themselves. They made a big deal out of going to the market. Ed dropped them off and Starr called him on his cellular when they were ready to be picked up. He didn't ask what they bought but they were excited and showed him what was in the bags when they got home. Of course, they bought more than they wanted to eat but still they ate more than either of them would have eaten on their own. Ed and Sara were balancing the power by giving it up.

Personally, I feared that Starr was going to make a big test of the ninety-pound weight requirement that would trigger the force-feeding at the clinic. Once she went two days without eating but by that time, she was enough above ninety pounds so that nothing happened. A few months later she tried it for four days, but they didn't worry because they were sure she was sneaking food. Ed and Sara were now at the point where they understood her every move and didn't give way to her various challenges.

The clinic reported that Starr was doing well and that her weight was up to ninety-five pounds. I advised them to tell the clinic not to report her weight to them so that there would be no chance they'd make a remark about any weight gain to Starr. More and more Ed and Sara began to get the idea that they had to drop completely out of the food and weight watching regimen they'd imposed on themselves for the last two years.

I am not saying that their love and concern led Starr to become anorexic. No one will ever know exactly why she chose to stop eating. But once a teenager gets involved in anorexia, it is extremely important not to allow her to ensnare her parents in this choice. Gradually, Ed and Sara extricated themselves from this trap. When they did, the pleasure that Starr got from controlling them ended. But sending her to the clinic was their insurance policy. Both they and Starr knew the clinicians would not let her starve herself to death.

There is one more point that did not come up in Starr's case, which is what they should do if the clinic called and told them that Starr had to be force-fed. At that point, Starr would use every trick in her large bag of tricks to keep that from happening. She would beg her parents to prevent the clinic from feeding her. She would promise to eat, even eat a big meal and then run to the bathroom and throw it up, telling them she couldn't help it. She'd threaten to kill herself or start talking crazy. She would accuse them of not loving her and of never having loved her. There would be no limit to what she would do to avoid losing control of what she had labored so hard to create.

It would be very difficult for her parents to resist her pressure. She would beg to be allowed to go down to eighty-eight pounds just for this one time. If her parents or the clinic gave in to any of her threats or promises, they would lose all they had worked for. Plus, by winning this battle, she might gain the strength she needed to starve herself to death. Parents of anorexics must keep in mind that they are not dealing with a rational person. An anorexic who is starving herself is choosing to play Russian roulette with her life. Not only should her parents not give in, unless the clinic has a reason not to force-feed her, they should tell her that they love her too much to give in.

If possible, they should stay with her as she is being fed and tell her that they love her too much to abandon her now. They should, however, not talk with her about the experience after it is over. Just tell her they are happy she is alive and that, if she wants to talk about the experience, there are professional counselors at the clinic who will be more than happy to talk with her about it.

Moreover, in such a scenario, she might use this experience to unload a lot of anger on her parents and they should try very hard not to respond with anger. They should keep telling her they love her, continue to talk about everything else that interested her, but not about food or eating.

When Starr finally gets over her desire to starve herself, there is always the chance that she might try another self-destructive activity like drugs, sex, school failure, or even craziness. Other chapters in this book deal with those possibilities. When she has recovered, she might also ask about why Ed and

Sara changed so abruptly, and this is a good time to tell her about choice theory and offer her this book to read and any of the other books listed in appendix A.

We live in an external control world that leads to the unhappiness we see all around us. As parents, you cannot escape from that world. But as much as you can, you can create a choice theory environment in your home and eliminate a lot of external control. Choice theory is a choice. I hope by now you are seriously considering it.

FIFTEEN

FRED'S BIG MEETING

I didn't hear from Fred after that last call. But when the time came for his appointment, I heard the chime in the waiting room and he was there. There was no doubt he was happy with the outcome of the meeting because there was a big smile on his face and he grabbed my hand and shook it. In his other hand he was clutching an audiotape. With some editing the following is the essence of the tape. As soon as his daughters spoke, he identified their voices, which were different enough so that I knew who was talking.

Fred started on the tape by saying, "It's like I told you, I want to have a talk." There was no response to this initial statement but Fred told me that at lunch he'd talked to them about what he wanted to do and they were waiting for him to go on. He then got things going by asking the following question: "I want you to tell me how you'd like me to treat you. I mean, I'm interested in what you think you'd like me to do. I'm puzzled. I want to be a good father. It'd help me a lot if you'd give me some idea of what I should do that would make you think I'm a good father?"

Then the voice he identified as Julia, the eighteen-year-old, said, "Come back home, back to Mom and to us." Two other voices chimed in, "Yeah, go back to Mom."

Fred handled it pretty well by saying, "That won't work.

I'm not a good husband. I don't think I can ever be a good husband to Mom and I don't even want to try. But I don't think I've been a good father, either. I want to try to be a better father. And if you'd help me, I think I could. Besides, I don't think Mom wants me back but I think she'd like me to be a better father than I've been. Would you guys help me?"

A younger voice that Fred identified as Kami, the thirteen-year-old, said, "I think you're a pretty good father. It's Julia, she's the one who keeps saying you're not."

The next voice was the fifteen-year-old, Lisa. "Julia says you're rich and you didn't leave Mom enough money. Are you rich, Dad?"

Julia chimed in, "He's rich, Lisa. He's loaded. He gave that bitch Rhonda a fortune and he didn't give Mom anything but a few bucks and child support. He's rich and we're poor."

"Julia, if I gave Mom some of the money she's asking for, would that make me a good father?"

"It'd help."

"Okay, I agree it'd help. But what I'm asking, I'm especially asking it of you, Julia, is what else do you want me to do that'd make me a better father?"

"Love us. When we come to see you, it seems you can't wait for us to go home."

The other two voices chimed in and said, "Yeah, Dad, love us. If you loved us, you'd never have left home for Rhonda."

"But Rhonda's gone. She's been gone for six years. I'm trying to love you. If I didn't love you, we wouldn't be having this talk. But I don't know how to show you I love you. I'm so scared I'm going to do something or say something wrong that I'm uncomfortable. And when I'm uncomfortable, you're uncomfortable. Do you see what I mean?"

Kami, the youngest, said, "Relax Dad, I love you."

"But that's the problem, I'm not relaxed. When I was home,

I mostly ignored you. I never learned how to relax and enjoy being with you."

Julia said, "You can say that again."

"That's what I mean. But I'm also trying to say that at home you have things to do that don't need me. Here with me, you don't know what to do and I don't know what to do with you. As soon as you come in, I feel as if I have to entertain you. I don't know how to entertain you. We've got to figure out a way for us to be together and for us to enjoy being together. Just me asking you that question . . . I can feel it, it makes you uncomfortable but what else can I do? You're not little girls that I can take to the park or out for a pony ride. I can give Mom every cent she's asking for; it still won't solve what we do when we get together."

Lisa said, "I think the problem's that all three of us are too much. We ought to come one at a time or maybe two at a time. But all three, it's too much for you."

Kami said, "That's a good idea. When we're home, it's never all three of us. Julia's never around. And Lisa's always with her friends."

Lisa said, "You're with your friends, too."

Fred said, "What do you think, Julia? Would you ever come to see me by yourself?"

Kami said, "Yeah, Julia, if we weren't here, you wouldn't be here. You'd never come. Why're you so mad at Dad?"

"I'm not mad at Dad. I just don't have anything to say to him. I don't know any girl my age, in college like I am, who talks to her father."

Lisa said, "You're mad at Dad. He's trying real hard to love us but you've made up your mind not to love him. It's selfish, it's making it hard on me and Kami."

Fred said, "Look, Julia. I love you. If you're mad at me, I

accept it. But I don't care how mad you are at me, I'm not going to stop loving you. I'm not going to stop loving any of you."

Julia started crying; I could hear it on the tape. She said, "I'm all confused. Mom talked to me about her problems being married to you. She didn't talk to Kami and Lisa, they were babies. Mom kept telling me that if you loved me, you never would have done what you did."

"Julia, I'm not going to say a word against Mom. Mom had a right to talk to you and tell you what a bad person I was. I was a bad person. A good father figures out a way to keep the family together and I didn't try hard enough. It was also sex. You're all old enough to know about sex. Sex makes people, especially men like me who think they're big deals, which makes them God's gift to women, do things they shouldn't do. It wasn't Mom's fault I left her. It wasn't even Rhonda's fault I left. It was my fault. But bad as I was, I never stopped loving any of you. But I've learned something about being out of the house for seven years. I've learned that none of you are babies. You don't need me to tell you what to do. I'm going to try to talk with you like I'm doing now. And listen to you like I am now. But I'm never going to tell any of you what to do with your life unless you ask me. I thought I knew everything when I left Mom. I didn't know anything. And right now, I don't have anyone in my life that I love except you. You can tell me anything or you can ask me for anything. You can spend time with me or you can stay away. Whatever you do, my job is to love you."

I could hear tears in Fred's voice as he finished that little speech.

Lisa said, "Mom always asks us what you say about her. When Kami and I tell her you don't say anything bad about her, she doesn't believe us. Julia doesn't say anything as long as we're around. You say if we play this tape, she'll see you don't talk against her, but I don't know. She's so mad at you that if we play this tape, she'll say that you did this whole thing to impress her, to try to get out of giving her more money. She says you're real clever. But I'll tell you, Dad, I never expected you to say anything like you just said. I'm not sure I want to play that tape for Mom. Maybe she's right. Do you really mean what you just said?"

Kami said, "What are you talking about, Lisa? Julia, what do you think?"

Fred said, "Go ahead, Julia, tell us what you think."

"I think that Dad should tell that to Mom right to her face in front of all of us. If he's trying to cheat her, Mom'll know."

"Julia, I'd be happy to play that tape for Mom in front of all of you. But Mom's mad at me and like I said, she has a right to be mad at me. But it's not what Mom thinks that counts with me. It's what you and Lisa think that counts. But if I come right out and ask you, it'll be putting you on the spot and I said I'd never do that. So I'm stuck. I know what I shouldn't do but I don't know what I should do."

Lisa started to answer but before she could say anything Julia started to talk. "Dad, I was almost Kami's age when you left. I was heartbroken. I saw how you treated Mom and how she treated you. I was aware that you and Mom had trouble getting along, long before you even met Rhonda. But what I couldn't figure out is why, all of a sudden, you wanted a divorce. I'd been to a lot of my girlfriends' houses and most of their parents don't get along much better than you and Mom. But most of them stayed together, most of them are still together, not that happy but not getting a divorce. There's something wrong with marriage, it's not happy after a while and no one seems to know what to do. I was aware that you and Mom were unhappy when I was four years old. I couldn't figure out why you went ahead and had two more kids. You kept telling me you wanted a boy but I never believed you. I'm living with a guy now. He's a nice guy and he's been talking about marriage. I'm not even nineteen years old and I told him he's crazy. His mom and dad have been divorced for years and remarried I don't know how many times. Listen to me. What am I saying? Is this what Kami and Lisa and me have to look forward to? Am I crazy or what?"

Fred whispered to me that both Kami and Lisa had been listening real close to what Julia was saying.

Kami then said, "Dad, it sounds like Julia's trying to tell you she doesn't even believe in love. But you know what I think? I think she's trying to tell you she loves you."

Lisa started to cry and said, "Kami's right. She loves you but she's afraid if she admits it that it'll turn out bad, that you won't love her. She's afraid, Dad, we're all afraid. But Julia's the most afraid. Dad, Julia really needs you."

Then I heard Fred saying over and over as he would if he were hugging Julia, "Julia, Julia, Julia baby, I love you. I love you."

There continued to be a lot of hugging and sobbing on the tape. I heard both Lisa and Kami telling Fred they loved him and they needed a hug, too. The tears were pouring down Fred's face when he cut off the tape.

He said to me, "I guess you've heard the story. I want to thank you. But I'd like to keep seeing you for a little while. Not often, maybe once a week for a couple months. There's going to be some backlash. Sandie will give the girls a hard time for giving in to me. I'm going to keep the tape but I have no intention of playing it for Sandie right now. Do you agree?"

"I agree. I don't know what else to say."

"But I can tell from your tone of voice, you're thinking of something. Tell me."

"I'm thinking you should try to resolve the money problem

as soon as you can. But I think you should explain all your thinking about money to your daughters and see if they'll go along with what you're going to do. How you do this is kind of tricky. It's as important that they're satisfied as Sandie."

"Can I talk to you about it?"

"You can, but I have to warn you, on the money issue I'm more on your family's side than I am on yours. I feel it's only fair to tell you that."

"It's okay. I figured that out the last time we met."

"I think we ought to talk about your love life, too. You said you're seeing a couple of women. If anything gets even the least bit serious, I think you'd be wise to bring the girls into that picture, too. It's the family stuff I'm concerned about, as I said last time."

I have a lawyer friend who deals with wealthy people's divorces. He tells me the children issue is by far the most bitter and difficult to solve. I hope this case will shed a little light on that most divisive problem. But the more important aspect of this chapter is for you to realize that many problems with teenagers could be avoided if the parents got along better.

When Fred read the material I gave him and realized the disastrous effects that external control, via the deadly habits, had on his marriage, he was appalled. But for his marriage it was too late. Fortunately, it was not too late for what he was able to do with his children.

From my vantage point as a psychiatrist, I have seen that marriage is the least successful of all human relationships and, if it weren't for divorce, the carnage, both real and psychological, of marriage failure would be mind-boggling. Like the weather, there is a lot of talk about improving marriage. But in my lifetime, nothing much has been done and there's no help visible on the horizon. It is my belief that even more than needing help as parents in getting along better with their children, married couples need to begin using choice theory much earlier in their marriage, and even before they get married.

To that end I suggest that all parents, married or single, read my book *Getting Together and Staying Together,** which explains how they can put choice theory to work in their relationships from the time they meet. As with all my books, there is no possibility of harm in using what I suggest but, from the letters I receive, many couples have gotten a lot of help from it.

If Fred and Sandie had had this information, the suffering that Julia described might not have occurred and Julia's belief in the hopelessness of marriage might not ever have entered her mind. There is evidence to support the idea that children of happily married couples have a better chance for marital success.

---

*All of Dr. Glasser's books, some coauthored with his wife, Carleen, are listed and annotated in appendix A.

Conclusion

In this book we have provided many examples of how to deal with unhappy teenagers. But there are also many problems we did not explicitly cover because to do so would have led to a lot of repetition. What we did provide was how to deal with any relationship problem: *Get rid of your use of external control and replace it with choice theory.* It is helpful if the other person in the relationship does the same, but as you have seen over and over in most of the chapters, if you do it, you can get the process started.

We live in an external control world but to the extent that you can create a choice theory environment in your own home, it has a very good chance of being picked up by your children. When they learn it, the power will be balanced because neither you nor they will now think in terms of power over the other. My suggestion: When you are having difficulty with your teenager, go back and reread the first two chapters of this book. Your difficulty will almost always be because either you or the teen is still using external control. You can't control what he or she is doing but you can control what you are doing, so redouble your efforts to learn to use choice theory.

Be patient. Both you and your teenager have been exposed to a lifetime of external control. It is very difficult to accept the choice theory idea that when you are dealing with another person you only know what's right for yourself and so can only control what you do. When you slip, as you will, correct yourself. If an apology is needed, apologize and go on.

Take it one day at a time and consider what you are going through, as if you were undergoing a recovery process very similar to one involved in giving up an addiction. In a sense you are trying to recover from a lifelong addiction to external control. It may not be as hard as recovering from drinking, smoking, or eating too much but it's far from easy. But there is a great difference between doing this and stopping an addiction. Whenever you succeed, you'll feel good. You won't miss the external control at all because what you are doing will feel so much better than what you've given up.

Good luck using what you've learned in this book. If you have a success, write and tell me about it (for contact information, see page 192). Accept that any failure you may have is only temporary. As long as your teenager is under your roof, if you persist in your effort to rid yourself of external control, your relationship will improve. Talk with your teenagers and tell them what you're trying to do. Pick out the chapter in the book closest to your situation and share it with them. Even if it's only for a few minutes, any honest conversation you have with your teenager that brings you closer together is a strong step in the right direction.

Appendix A

Further reading material that may be valuable both for parents of adolescents and for therapists who work with them is listed below.

Unless otherwise noted, the following books by William Glasser, M.D., are available or can be ordered at most bookstores and online from Amazon.com. Some of the books are coauthored with his wife, Carleen Glasser. All Glasser books can be ordered directly from William Glasser Inc., which is housed at the William Glasser Institute (see appendix B). To obtain pricing information on the books, refer to the institute's Web site: www.wglasser.com.

Choice Theory: A New Psychology of Personal Freedom, 1998. This is the basic book on choice theory psychology. It explains the theory and how it differs markedly from the destructive world psychology that Dr. Glasser calls external control psychology. It is explained in a way that will allow the reader to begin to use it in every aspect of his or her life.

Counseling with Choice Theory: The New Reality Therapy, 2001. In this updated and expanded edition of his bestselling 1965 book, *Reality Therapy*, Dr. Glasser initiated the way he now presents cases. The reader sits with him, listens to what he says, why he says it, and what the client says. This book helps the reader to understand more about how Dr. Glasser deals with a wide variety of psychological problems.

The Language of Choice Theory, 2000.
This book explains how to use choice theory to replace external control as parents talk to their children, husbands and wives talk to each other, teachers talk to students, and managers talk to workers. This book brings the difference between choice theory and external control to life. Readers will recognize themselves and all the people they know in its many examples.

Getting Together and Staying Together, 2000.
Here choice theory is applied to finding a mate and living happily after marriage. Dr. and Mrs. Glasser explain how they use these ideas in their own marriage. This book also provides insights into the reasons for unhappy marriages and creative solutions for putting the happiness back in.

What Is This Thing Called Love? The Essential Book for the Single Woman, 2000.
Single women learn how to apply choice theory to their relationships, especially how to deal with a man who is reluctant to commit to marriage. For those who have had a bad experience with a man who professes love, this book provides new information and understanding.

Fibromyalgia: Hope from a Completely New Perspective, 2001.
This book applies choice theory to the condition or "disease" called fibromyalgia. It is included here because this painful condition is often related to an unsatisfying relationship between a parent and a teenage child.

The following book is available only through William Glasser Inc. at the Willliam Glasser Institute (see appendix B):

Every Student Can Succeed, 2000.
This book applies choice theory to the classroom and explains how every student can succeed. For parents, teachers, and teacher educators.

If you or your child or adolescent is on psychiatric medication, the following books explain that there is no pathology in the brains of people who are now diagnosed with what are called mental illnesses unless the pathology is obvious, as in Alzheimer's disease. They are available in all bookstores.

Peter Breggin, M.D. *Toxic Psychiatry.* New York: St. Martin's Press, 1991.
Through his painstaking review of psychiatric research, Dr. Breggin explains that there is no pathology in the brain and that mental illness, even what is now labeled schizophrenia and clinical depression, can be as successfully treated with caring psychotherapy as it can with potentially harmful psychiatric drugs.

Peter Breggin, M.D., and David Cohen, Ph.D., *Your Drug May Be Your Problem: How and Why to Stop Taking Psychiatric Medications.* New York: HarperCollins/Perseus Books, 1999.
This book documents the dangers of taking psychiatric drugs for all conditions. It is well worth reading for those who are on any psychiatric medication and are not getting the expected benefit from it.

Appendix B

In 1967, I founded the Institute for Reality Therapy for the purpose of teaching that approach to counselors, educators, managers, and literally anyone who worked with people. Since its inception, I have greatly expanded my thinking with the addition of choice theory and have applied that theory to almost every aspect of reality therapy. I have also extended the use of choice theory into the schools, as exemplified by the quality school program, and into managing for quality in all other areas in which people are managed. My ideas are being applied to an entire community in Corning, New York.

With all these expansions and applications, I have gone so far beyond reality therapy that, for accuracy, I was encouraged to change the name of the institute to the William Glasser Institute. In 1996 I made the change so that anyone who is interested in any of my ideas and their application could easily contact us. Over the years, as our teaching and training have expanded, satellite organizations have been set up in many countries around the world.

The institute, under the leadership of Linda Harshman, coordinates and monitors all training and serves as an information clearinghouse. My latest thinking is often made available through audiotapes, videotapes, and publications. The *International Journal of Reality Therapy*, produced at Northeastern

University, is the research arm of the institute and serves as a vehicle through which its members can publish their works on new ways of using and teaching reality therapy.

As mentioned, the basic purpose of the William Glasser Institute is to provide training for professionals who want to use my ideas in their work with others. There are five parts to this training, which takes a minimum of eighteen months to complete: Basic Intensive Week, Basic Practicum, Advanced Intensive Week, Advanced Practicum, and the Certification Week. All of the instruction is done in small groups, and by explanation, discussion, and demonstration. Upon successful completion of the process, the individual is awarded a certificate that states he or she is Reality Therapy Certified. The certificate is not a license to practice counseling or psychotherapy. These practices are governed by the appropriate licensing authorities in various legal jurisdictions in North America and in other countries.

The institute employs user-friendly people trained in choice theory, so if you contact us, you can be sure of a courteous response. It is my vision to teach choice theory to the world. I invite you to join me in this effort.

For further information about my work, including my lectures, books, and audio and video materials as well as the institute programs, contact:

The William Glasser Institute
22024 Lassen Street, Suite 118
Chatsworth, CA 91311
Phone: 800-899-0688; 818-700-8000
Fax: 818-700-0555
E-mail: wginst@earthlink.net
Web: www.wglasser.com

INDEX